THE THREAT OF LIBERATION

The Threat of Liberation

Imperialism and Revolution in Zanzibar

Amrit Wilson

First published 2013 by Pluto Press
345 Archway Road, London N6 5AA

www.plutobooks.com

Copyright © Amrit Wilson 2013

The right of Amrit Wilson to be identified as the author of this work has been asserted by her in accordance with the Copyright, Designs and Patents Act 1988.

British Library Cataloguing in Publication Data
A catalogue record for this book is available from the British Library

ISBN 978 0 7453 3408 0 Hardback
ISBN 978 0 7453 3407 3 Paperback
ISBN 978 1 8496 4939 1 PDF eBook
ISBN 978 1 8496 4941 4 Kindle eBook
ISBN 978 1 8496 4940 7 EPUB eBook

Library of Congress Cataloging in Publication Data applied for

This book is printed on paper suitable for recycling and made from fully managed and sustained forest sources. Logging, pulping and manufacturing processes are expected to conform to the environmental standards of the country of origin.

10 9 8 7 6 5 4 3 2 1

Typeset by Curran Publishing Services, Norwich

Every effort has been made to trace copyright holders and to obtain their permission for the use of the photographs in this book. The publisher apologises for any errors or omissions in this respect and would be grateful if notified of any corrections that should be incorporated in future reprints or editions.

Contents

List of photographs   viii
Acknowledgements   x
List of acronyms and abbreviations   xi

Introduction   1

1 **Anti-Colonial Struggles – The Early Days**   11
   Zanzibar: Ethnicity, Class and the Shadows of the Past   12
   Anti-Colonial Struggle and the First Nationalist Party   15
   British Fears and the Formation of the Afro-Shirazi Party   17
   Revolutionary Sparks in the Air of Zanzibar   19
   Racial Tensions: The Pan African Movement Intervenes   26
   An Opportunistic Alliance of the Right   29
   Strategies of the Left in a Reactionary Climate   32

2 **The British Transfer Power to the Sultan and His Allies**   35
   The British, the ZNP–ZPPP Alliance, and Dirty Tricks   35
   What Makes Someone Guilty of Sedition?   37
   The Lancaster House Constitutional Conference   39
   A Revolutionary Party Is Launched   41

3 **The Zanzibar Revolution and Imperialist Fears**   46
   'A Week of Grievous Shame for the Nation'   49
   The United States Formulates New Strategies for Africa   51
   Early Days of the People's Republic of Zanzibar   52
   'Racial Strategy Acted Out on Women's Bodies'   55
   The Demise of the Legal System   56
   The Dissolution of the Umma Party   57
   The Zanzibar that Might Have Been   58

4 **The Union with Tanganiyka**   61
   Nyerere's Progressive Cult   62

CONTENTS

	Karume Signs Away the People's Republic of Zanzibar	64
	Early Days of Tanzania – the Mainland	65
	Nyerere's Acolytes 'Look After' the Left	65
	The Tanzania–Zambia rail link, TAZARA	68
	Economic Policies: Differences between Babu and Nyerere	71
5	**Karume's Despotic Rule**	**77**
	Karume Hands Military Power to his Henchmen	78
	Days of Violence and Tyranny	79
	Karume's Assasination and its Aftermath	82
	Arrests, Incarceration and Torture on the Mainland	84
6	**Trial in Zanzibar's Kangaroo Court**	**90**
	The Trial	90
	The Long Years in Prison	94
	The Campaign for the Release of Babu and All Political Prisoners	95
7	**Zanzibar and the Mainland in the Neoliberal Era**	**100**
	'Development' in Zanzibar and Mainland Tanzania Today	102
	Aid and Dependency	106
	'The Jewel in the Crown of Tanzania'	107
	US Fears of China	110
	US Fears About Iran	112
8	**US Interventions in Zanzibar and on the Mainland Today**	**114**
	The US Military's Role in Tanzania	117
	The East African Community and the War on Terror	119
	Building 'Sources' and 'Resources'	122
	'Militant Youth' and the Government of National Unity	123
	Diplomats and Donors Try to Play 'Hard Ball'	126
	Zanzibar and the Future	129

Appendices:
1 A People's Programme: The Political Programme and
   Constitution of the Umma Party   139

CONTENTS

2 Charge Sheet: Case no. 292 of 1973 (the Umma Defendants)   149

Notes   *157*
References   *160*
Index   *171*

Photographs

1. Babu soon after his return from London in 1957 — 21
2. Schoolgirl members of YOU photographed by the British anxious about 'militant youth' — 23
3. Accra, All African People's Conference 1958 — 29
4. Babu arriving at a celebration on April 29, 1963 to mark his release from jail — 40
5. A huge crowd eagerly waiting to welcome Babu in front of the ZNP headquarters at Darajani — 41
6. Babu with Karume — 50
7. Che Guevara and Babu, relaxing after the first UNCTAD conference in Geneva, July 1964 — 53
8. Malcolm X and Babu — 68
9. Signing of a trade agreement and a protocol concerning the exchange of commodities between China and Tanzania on February 10, 1965 — 69
10. Babu and Vice President Kawawa with heroes of the long march, January 1965 — 70
11. In the Great Hall of the People, Beijing, 1965 — 71
12. Babu trying to explain his economic approach to Nyerere — 72
13. Release of the Umma comrades on the mainland — 97

PHOTOGRAPHS

14 Babu with Tajudeen Abdulraheem General Secretary of the Seventh Pan African Congress, and other young activists of the Pan African Movement, March 1994   98

15 Qullatein Badawi, Hashil Seif Hashil and Khamis Ameir in Zanzibar on June 28, 2011   136

Acknowledgements

This book is in many ways a collective effort, written by me but conceived and thought through by my comrades Khamis Ameir, Shaaban Salim and Hamed Hilal, who were all cadres of the Umma Party. It was they who not only related their experiences but collected data and pictures and explained events to me. It is their book as much as mine, although I alone am responsible for any errors.

I would also like to remember our dear comrade the late Qullatein Badawi, who supported and encouraged us in our efforts at researching this book, and thank Hashil Seif Hashil, also once an Umma cadre, for sharing his experiences with me.

In the period when I actually wrote this book, Narendra Gajjar was the person I turned to most frequently. He made sure he was always ready to respond by phone or email to my queries, unhesitatingly providing contacts, interesting documents and suggestions on how to approach tricky interviewees.

Among the many others whose help I would like to acknowledge are Mohamed Saleh and Salma Maoulidi for providing me with their writings, Mailys Chauvin for helping me check various facts during her stay in Zanzibar and allowing me to use her photograph of Khamis, Badawi and Hashil taken in 2012, and Firoze Manji for his encouragement at a time when I was unsure whether my manuscript could ever become a book.

Thanks are also due to the team at Pluto Press and especially Anne Beech for her support and her sensitive and painstaking editing.

Finally I would like to thank my family for reading and commenting on many of the chapters which follow – without their enthusiasm and support I could never have completed this book.

Amrit Wilson

PHOTOGRAPHS

14 Babu with Tajudeen Abdulraheem General Secretary
    of the Seventh Pan African Congress, and other young
    activists of the Pan African Movement, March 1994   98

15 Qullatein Badawi, Hashil Seif Hashil and Khamis
    Ameir in Zanzibar on June 28, 2011   136

Acknowledgements

This book is in many ways a collective effort, written by me but conceived and thought through by my comrades Khamis Ameir, Shaaban Salim and Hamed Hilal, who were all cadres of the Umma Party. It was they who not only related their experiences but collected data and pictures and explained events to me. It is their book as much as mine, although I alone am responsible for any errors.

I would also like to remember our dear comrade the late Qullatein Badawi, who supported and encouraged us in our efforts at researching this book, and thank Hashil Seif Hashil, also once an Umma cadre, for sharing his experiences with me.

In the period when I actually wrote this book, Narendra Gajjar was the person I turned to most frequently. He made sure he was always ready to respond by phone or email to my queries, unhesitatingly providing contacts, interesting documents and suggestions on how to approach tricky interviewees.

Among the many others whose help I would like to acknowledge are Mohamed Saleh and Salma Maoulidi for providing me with their writings, Mailys Chauvin for helping me check various facts during her stay in Zanzibar and allowing me to use her photograph of Khamis, Badawi and Hashil taken in 2012, and Firoze Manji for his encouragement at a time when I was unsure whether my manuscript could ever become a book.

Thanks are also due to the team at Pluto Press and especially Anne Beech for her support and her sensitive and painstaking editing.

Finally I would like to thank my family for reading and commenting on many of the chapters which follow – without their enthusiasm and support I could never have completed this book.

Amrit Wilson

Acronyms and abbreviations

AAPC	All African People's Conference
AFRICOM	United States Africa Command
AGA	AngloGold Ashanti
AIMP	Association for Islamic Mobilization and Propagation
ANC	African National Congress
AOPIG	African Oil Policy Initiative Group
ASP	Afro-Shirazi Party
ASU	Afro-Shirazi Union
ATA	Anti-Terrorism Assistance
CCM	Chama cha Mapinduzi
CIA	(US) Central Intelligence Agency
CMOs	Civil Military Operations
CT	counterterrorism
CUF	Civic United Front
DCM	deputy chief of mission
DfID	Department for International Development (UK)
DRC	Democratic Republic of Congo
EAC	East African Community
EALA	East African Legislative Assembly
EPZ	export processing zone
FDI	foreign direct investment
FPTU	Federation of Progressive Trade Unions
FRTU	Federation of Revolutionary Trade Unions
GOT	Government of Tanzania
ICFTU	International Confederation of Free Trade Unions
IMF	International Monetary Fund
MIGA	Multilateral Investment Guarantee Agency
MOU	memorandum of understanding
MPLA	People's Movement for the Liberation of Angola
NASA	National Aeronautics and Space Administration (USA)
NGO	non-government organization

ACRONYMS AND ABBREVIATIONS

NPT	Non-Proliferation Treaty
OAU	Organization of African Unity
PAC	Pan Africanist Congress
PAFMECA	Pan African Freedom Movement of East and Central Africa
PLA	People's Liberation Army
PNUSS	Party of National Unity for the Sultan's Subjects
REDET	Research and Education for Democracy in Tanzania
SEZ	special economic zones
SWAPO	South West Africa People's Organization
TANU	Tanganyika African National Union
TAZARA	Tanzania–Zambia railway
tcf	trillion cubic feet
TIC	Tanzanian Investment Center
TPDC	Tanzania Petroleum Development Corporation
TPDF	Tanzanian People's Defense Force
UNCTAD	United Nations Conference on Trade and Development
UNDP	United Nations Development Programme
URTZ	United Republic of Tanganyika and Zanzibar
YOU	Youths Own Union
ZAPU	Zimbabwe African People's Union
ZNP	Zanzibar Nationalist Party
ZPFL	Zanzibar and Pemba Federation of Labour
ZPFTU	Zanzibar and Pemba Federation of Trade Unions
ZPPP	Zanzibar and Pemba People's Party

*In memory of Babu
and for the people of Zanzibar
whose struggle continues*

Introduction

A place of 'tailor made adventures', and 'ecological safaris', 'a paradise whose very name evokes intrigue': these are some of the most common descriptions of Zanzibar today. Increasingly, over the first decade of the 2000s, the Isles, as Zanzibar's two islands (Unguja and Pemba) are often called, have been sold as a playground for western tourists. This is a place, we are being asked to believe, that begins and ends in the present, with neither a past of any political relevance nor a future any different from today. Even its history is available in pill form, neatly packaged for tourist consumption.

But as in the case of many such 'paradises', the reality for people who live there is very different. For them multiple layers of memory and history continue to intrude into the present. On the ferry which takes people from Dar es Salaam to Unguja and back, a group of young men argue animatedly about the Zanzibar revolution of 1964 and its aftermath, about the effects of Zanzibar's union with Tanganyika to form Tanzania which followed, and the roles of Julius Nyerere, Abdulrahman Mohamed Babu and Abeid Karume. In the daily newspapers, the events of the 1960s and 1970s lead to heated debates. The bitterness of those who lost their loved ones and often their livelihoods in the period which saw the subversion and tragic aftermath of the revolution surfaces in a multitude of comments, discussions, memoirs and blogs. And in the coffee shops, those who do not owe allegiance to either of the two political parties, the Chama cha Mapinduzi (CCM) and Civic United Front (CUF), joke about the three-year-old and already fractious 'Government of national unity' put in place under pressure from the West. Tragedy, they say, is being repeated as farce. Meanwhile, everyone is aware of the presence of the US army. They are opening schools, conferring awards, and entrenching themselves on the islands, because as secret documents revealed by Wikileaks show, today, as at the time of the 1964 revolution and the Cold War, Zanzibar is once again seen as an important piece in the jigsaw of the United States's foreign and military policy in Africa.

US intervention in Zanzibar after the revolution had many things in common with more recent US interventions in Africa. In fact, many aspects of the model created during the Cold War are still in use today. Like the Libyan uprising, in Zanzibar too the United States went all out to make it seem like an 'African initiative'. But while NATO intervened and invaded Libya to fight Gaddafi's forces, in Zanzibar the United States pushed the British to intervene, and formulated a Zanzibar Action Plan under which they would work on the leaders they could manipulate to ask for a British military intervention.

That such an intervention did not occur during or immediately after the Zanzibar uprising was, perhaps at least partly because of the presence of a well-organized revolutionary party, the Umma Party. Although it did not start the revolution, Umma turned it from a lumpen uprising into a revolutionary insurrection, and took over state power to secure it within hours. As for the nature of the revolution itself, in many ways it was the first of its kind in modern Africa. Whereas African countries with the exception of Kenya and Algeria had become independent through a process of negotiated decolonization (in Zanzibar the British had handed over power to the Sultan), the Zanzibar revolution was the first time a neocolonial administration had been overthrown. Here, as Babu, leader of the Umma Party, was to write, the people rose up not simply to 'overthrow a politically bankrupt government and a caricature monarchy. They revolted in order to change the social system which had oppressed them and for once to take the destiny of their history into their own hands' (Babu, 1989: 3).

The pages that follow trace the path of the Umma Party and its cadres, using testimonies and historic photographs, interviews, and formerly secret US and British documents. We examine how the party emerged from the thick of anti-colonial mobilizations to confront the rulers to whom the British had transferred power at independence, and how it evolved strategies for unity in the face of an ethnically divided Zanzibar. (See Chapter 1 for a discussion of ethnicity and class in Zanzibar.)

Through the experiences of Umma cadres, many of whom were trained in Cuba and in Nasser's Egypt, we look at what happened in the revolution itself, how they secured it by taking over the institutions of the state, and how their very presence (they included not only a large number of Arabs but also Africans and Indians) prevented anti-Arab violence from becoming the central thrust of the revolution.

INTRODUCTION

'There was chaos everywhere,' as Hashil Seif Hashil, who was on the Central Committee of Umma Youth, recollected: 'Many people just did not know what they were doing. One of the things which the Umma Party did was to explain the purpose of the revolution – it was not to kill, rape or steal but to change the country. Some people listened but obviously not everyone' (quoted in Wilson, 1989: 12).

Through the eyes of Umma Party cadres we also look at the period following the revolution, the setting-up of the new revolutionary government in an alliance between the Umma Party and the Afro-Shirazi Party (ASP), an organization beset with contradictions, and the three months which ended in the subversion of the revolution. In this period, behind the scenes, the United States and the United Kingdom planned an invasion of Zanzibar, plotted to assassinate Babu, and did everything they could to create divisions within the new government. The conflict that emerged within the revolutionary government led to the dissolution of the Umma Party, but the cadres stayed together and acted for many purposes as a group.

The United States and the United Kingdom finally succeeded in 'neutralizing' Zanzibar and crushing its progressive potential by engineering the union of Zanzibar and Tanganyika to create a new country, Tanzania, presided over by a man they could trust, the pro-western Nyerere. It was a union that was achieved by subterfuge, bypassing accepted legal procedure and without consulting the people of either country. It was done with the connivance of pro-western leaders of Tanganyika, Kenya and Uganda.

The situation in Zanzibar deteriorated particularly after the Union, and Karume, the leader of the ASP, began to rule the islands like his personal fiefdom, killing, torturing and incarcerating those who disagreed with his policies or stood up to him. We follow these years of suffering through the experiences of some of the Umma cadres – those incarcerated and tortured in Zanzibar as well as on the mainland.

The Union was conceived and achieved in secret, but much of the process was recorded in detail, if inadvertently, by the CIA and the US State Department, whose documents reveal not only the contempt in which the Americans held African leaders but the extent of their own deceit and unscrupulousness. They not only planned assassinations but offered bribes and bolstered those like Nyerere whom they could control. In January 1964, for example, just eight days after the revolution, G. Mennen Williams, US assistant secretary of state for

East Africa, was telling the US secretary of state in a secret memorandum, 'Our central purpose is to strengthen the position of Nyerere ... Nyerere may well need elements of a new program to assert his power' (quoted in Wilson, 1989: 27).

Such was the fear generated in the US State Department by the revolution in these small islands that within weeks the Americans had flown in one of their most experienced CIA operatives to Zanzibar. Frank Carlucci, who was later defense secretary under Ronald Reagan, arrived straight from the Congo where the CIA had been deeply involved in the overthrow of Lumumba. In Carlucci's words, the United States had to neutralize socialist elements in Zanzibar, because 'had there not been the Union, Zanzibar would have been an African Cuba from which sedition would spread to the continent' (quoted in Wilson, 1987). In a forerunner to today's AFRICOM policy, the United States began to plan a so-called 'belt of control' strategy, under which Central and East Africa (including Zanzibar) would be brought under its control, to prevent socialist influences from North Africa reaching the countries of Southern Africa and endangering their western investments.

The declassified US cables and UK government documents from the 1960s show some striking continuities and differences with those of the last few years exposed by Wikileaks. There is the same continuous intelligence gathering (only the 'sources' of today are not only politicians but also Tanzanian army officials and non-government organizations, NGOs); the same anxieties about the youth, who in the 1960s had been 'drilling and training in what can only be described as a militant manner' (HMSO, 1961: 3) and today are involved according to US cables in 'angry outbursts' which 'bears careful watching' (US Embassy, 2006b), and the same fear of Zanzibar becoming part of a crucial network of US enemies. The bogeymen, however, are very different; whereas once they were communists, today they are 'Islamic terrorists'.

Compare, for example, Carlucci's comment above with these concerns from the US Embassy in Dar es Salaam in a secret policy paper in July 2008:

> Zanzibaris are among the al-Queda [sic] members involved in the 1998 attack on this mission. There are pockets of extremist support throughout the Swahili cultural region (the coasts of Kenya and

Tanzania, Zanzibar and the Swahilophone Comoros islands). The reservoir of unemployed, desperate, hopeless, angry and alienated Islamic youth for terrorists to recruit from is greater in Zanzibar than elsewhere in the Swahili cultural area. Family and commercial links within the Swahili world are such that repercussions of events in one place are felt elsewhere in the region. Increased radicalization in Zanzibar would infect the whole region.

(US Embassy, 2008a)

The Cold War scenario meant that the United States was convinced that China, or the 'Chicoms' as the Americans called the Chinese, were behind every change in the weather.

The China of that period was a very different country from what it is today. It provided both inspiration and a model for a host of anti-colonial struggles across Africa and Asia. China had emerged 'through its own efforts', as Babu wrote, 'and against all odds, into a contender for world leadership. It evoked all the emotions of joy and hope for the oppressed who were still struggling under very difficult circumstances' (Babu, 1996: 327).

China's experiences demonstrated both the need for economic nationalism and the broad strategies for developing a self-reliant economy (ideas that are relevant once again in the current era of new colonial wars). They influenced the blueprint for a self-reliant economy which was in the process of being implemented in Zanzibar, when the forces of counter-revolution engineered the Union.

However China, despite its influence, had no direct role in the uprising, and like the elusive weapons of mass destruction in Iraq, the US officials searched and searched but could not find any Chinese weapons. Nevertheless they told each other in secret communiqués that 'Although documentary proof not available, circumstantial evidence of Chicom involvement in [the] Zanzibar revolt ... points strongly to Chicom participation in financing and planning the coup ... there is no hard evidence yet' (quoted in Wilson, 1989: 37).

The US fear of China's influence has not gone away. In fact it has come back in a powerful new incarnation as China and the United States compete for Africa's natural resources, particularly oil.

China has, so far, been willing to obtain its resources through trade, providing light industrial goods in return for raw materials, and building and developing infrastructure – railways and bridges, for example – to facilitate this process.

The US strategy in Africa today is very different. It has involved military conquest, regime change and the setting-up or strengthening of pro-US governments (like that of Tanzania) which help the siphoning-off of resources to the United States and Europe. However, the US army in Africa wishes to be regarded as a 'friendly' force. In Tanzania, for example, a secret US Embassy document in June 2009 noted that some thee years earlier, the government of Tanzania had agreed to the establishment of a Civil Affairs presence on the Swahili Coast by the US Combined Joint Task Force–Horn of Africa. This 'Civil Affairs team (which we have rebranded as "AFRICOM") is carrying out humanitarian projects and helping build Civil Military Operations (CMOs) … capacity within the Tanzania Peoples Defense Forces (TPDF)' (US Embassy, 2009a).

Civil Military Operations (CMOs) involve the US military working with the administration and NGOs (see page 118) to carry out surveillance, abduction, rendition and torture, and various military actions, to deal with 'sharpening competition/exploitation of dwindling natural resources' and other 'potential challenges' to the United States (US Joint Chiefs of Staff, 2008).

The US Congressional Research Services provide us with more specific information about the 'brand name' AFRICOM. Essentially an organization that unifies and coordinates the US military across Africa, AFRICOM was set up in 2008 under the Bush Administration to 'promote U.S. national security objectives in Africa and its surrounding waters'. It reflected an overtly colonial approach towards Africa, summed up by the Bush National Security Strategy of 2002: 'In Africa, promise and opportunity sit side by side with disease, war, and desperate poverty. This threatens both a core value of the United States – preserving human dignity – and our strategic priority – combating global terror' (Bush, 2002).

However, although it was projected as 'combating global terror', one of AFRICOM's key underlying purposes is containing Chinese influence, denying China access to oil and other resources, and taking them over for the United States. That is also what the United States was doing in Libya (Engdahl, 2011).

As Patrick Henningsen writes:

> The transnational corporate capture and control of the world's remaining resources and energy supplies will be … fought through

INTRODUCTION

numerous proxies, and on far-flung pitches across the globe but it will never be spoken of by the White House Press Secretary or the Foreign Office in Downing Street.

(Henningsen, 2011)

What will be spoken of instead will be the details of fabricated scenarios which demand US intervention for 'moral reasons', for example 'humanitarian intervention' as in the invasion of Libya and earlier in Somalia, neutralizing weapons of mass destruction and bringing democracy as in Iraq and more recently in Iran, or by invoking the War on Terror as in Afghanistan and in Somalia today.

It is in this latter context that Zanzibar is regarded as part of a strategic region, extending from the Horn of Africa and the Arabian peninsula to Ethiopia and the Seychelles via Kenya. It is here that the War on Terror has been pursued over the last couple of decades, and it is likely to intensify. It is in this area of countries bordering the Indian Ocean that secret drone airbases are being established (Channel 4 News, 2011), in order to target any East African country that does not allow the United States access to its natural resources. It is from here that these pilotless aircraft are taking off and flying across Africa to target unarmed populations, killing men, women and children whose names are simply forgotten and whose deaths amount to nothing more than 'collateral damage': see for example Press TV (2012).

Almost every country in East Africa is rich in the resources that the United States are seeking. Today it is Somalia (with its oil fields and its uranium) that is being targeted in a second phase of attacks; tomorrow it could be Sudan again in round two, and at some time in the future it may even be Zanzibar with its oil and gas deposits. In the 1990s the action in Somalia was supposedly about humanitarian relief for famine victims which was being blocked by 'warlords'. Today it is about fighting terrorism by al-Shabaab; tomorrow, it could be a different terrorist group. The War on Terror can always find 'terrorists'. They could be ordinary people going about their business which happens to stand in the way of corporate loot, or they could be organizations that grow under the shadow of imperialism – generated by people's anger against its injustices or in some cases encouraged and created by imperialism itself, but always in regions rich in resources.

Barack Obama made clear in the preamble to his statement on defence cuts that 'access' is what the United States is seeking. 'As we …

reshape our Armed Forces, we will ... continue to invest in the capabilities critical to future success, including intelligence, surveillance, and reconnaissance; counterterrorism; countering weapons of mass destruction; operating in anti-access environments' (US Department of Defense, 2012). His statement on 'defense cuts', also confirms 'strategic partnerships' with African armies. This means that wars in Africa will continue to be fought using the armies of countries like Ethiopia, Kenya and increasingly Tanzania. Unless there is a major challenge to imperialism, the future will see more of this, and it will be Africans who are killed and African soldiers who both kill and die to secure resources for the United States.

As for the War on Terror, it has proved too useful to the United States for it to be abandoned, and Obama's statement makes it clear that it will continue – carried out, as we know, through 'renditions', 'terminations' and 'targeted killings'. In Tanzania (as in Kenya), it is in any case well established, with the Kikwete government deeply involved in it for more than a decade. As far back as 2003, the government was carrying out abduction and 'extraordinary rendition' under US orders. One shocking case of a man abducted, flown across the world to one of the CIA's so-called 'black sites' (Interights, 2011), tortured and released three years later without being charged, is currently before the African Commission on Human and People's Rights. Where these activities have been publicly exposed, US officials justify them in the name of fighting terrorism in East Africa, invoking not only the bombings of the US Embassies in Dar and Nairobi (which are believed to have been revenge for American involvement in the extradition, and alleged torture, of four members of the Egyptian Islamic Jihad arrested in Albania), but increasingly over the last few years pointing to the activities of al-Shabaab.

The creation of Tanzania by the British and Americans has led in Zanzibar to half a century of stagnation, during which it has been subsumed into the underdeveloped mainland of Tanzania and the administration has all but destroyed its productive forces. Since the multiparty system was established in Tanzania 1992, Zanzibar's two political parties, whose support comes from the same electoral bases as were involved on opposite sides in the 1950s, leading to the 1964 revolution, have remained polarized as before. However, they are now joined in a government of national unity. But what does such a government mean under these circumstances, and why did the United States and Europe cajole and threaten the two warring parties to form it? What was the reason for this diplomatic and political intervention by the West? As the Wikileaks documents show, it was done to blunt the threat to imperialist control represented by the anger of the oppressed, the unemployed and the youth who see no future. It was engineered, in other words, to provide a stable environment both in Zanzibar and in mainland Tanzania, where transnational companies would be able to get to work appropriating this part of Africa's rich resources.

As we go to press Zanzibar stands at a critical moment when the nature of the Union is being discussed – and not just the politicians but the people are to have a say. What kind of Zanzibar do the youth and struggling people of Zanzibar want? Will their voices be heard? The history of Zanzibar over the last half century shows two essential principles. The first is the need for unity – a genuine unity which moves on from the mutual suspicion which has plagued the Isles and builds a new politics – and the second is an awareness of and opposition to imperialism with its wars and its ruthless looting. On these islands, as elsewhere in Africa, imperialism has been resisted before. It can and must be resisted again.

CHAPTER ONE

Anti-Colonial Struggles – The Early Days

The mid-1950s and early 1960s, when this story begins, had a number of striking similarities with today. In Africa, the United States and the United Kingdom were seeking desperately to institute 'regime change' and bring in governments that they could manipulate and use in their own interests. They were using covert methods and ideologies of fear, whipping up paranoia and unleashing witch hunts – but at that time against communists, not 'Islamic terrorists'. In their plan for continuing to exploit the countries of Africa (many of which were either newly independent or fighting colonialism), Zanzibar was regarded as a crucial place. The United States saw it as part of a Central African belt which, if controlled, would protect Southern Africa (with its western investments) from the radical and socialist influences of countries like Algeria and Ghana. If Zanzibar went out of this orbit, they feared, the whole of Africa might follow.

Zanzibar was and still is a remarkable place. A hub of commerce for two thousand years connecting Asia, Africa and the Arabian peninsula, it was, as it were, a cosmopolitan centre of the world. Historian Abdul Sheriff describes evocatively what Zanzibar town was like in his childhood in the early 1950s when he played on the narrow streets with kids who were Swahili, Omani, Persian, Hadhrami or Indian in origin, and how every monsoon saw the arrival of 'dhows and sailors from Arabia, the Persian Gulf, India and Somalia … the harbour was also full of coasting *Jahazis* from Lamu and Kilwa. There was a great intermingling of peoples' (Sheriff, 2008).

This multicultural scene also reflected a vibrant anti-imperialism which came out of the experiences of the Second World War and shaped the consciousness of many of the nationalists and revolutionaries of the 1950s and 1960s. During the war, as Abdulrahman Mohamed Babu wrote:

> Many young Zanzibaris were drafted to fight in British armies, mostly in Africa and Asia...in the post-war period they returned from the war zones bringing back the reality and scale of imperialist violence. Their stories of meeting recruits from other colonies (especially those from the 'Gold Coast', now Ghana, in the Burma campaign) helped make us in Zanzibar aware of the possibilities of solidarity and revolution.
> (Babu, 1996)

Zanzibar: Ethnicity, Class and the Shadows of the Past

How did the social structure of these islands develop? From 1830s on they had been ruled by a dynasty of Sultans who, while they originated in Oman, had settled in Zanzibar intermarrying with local people, speaking Swahili and by the mid-20th century hardly speaking Arabic at all. In addition, because of its unique position, Zanzibar had faced a series of colonial incursions by the Portuguese, Omanis, Germans and French, and finally, in 1890, by the British.

It was a partly as a by-product of these colonial experiences that Zanzibar became a society riven with contradictions, with a strong cultural unity on the one hand and deep ethnic divisions on the other, divisions whose shadow still haunts the Isles today. Zanzibar's history as a centre of commerce, and the fact that it was an entrepôt for goods going to and coming from the interior of Africa had led it to be drawn into the acquisition and transport of slaves, although the numbers involved here were far smaller than those involved in the Transatlantic slave trade.[1] At the same time, the growing interest of the imperialist powers in the Isles in the 19th century coincided with the introduction of cloves to Zanzibar. 'The subsequent development of a plantation system, deeply affected the relations of production on the island. The slaves that were taken from the continent were no longer solely a trade item [but] a source of productive labour on the plantations' (Depelchin, 1991: 14). At that point Zanzibar became a slave society, and it continued to be so till slavery was abolished in Unguja and Pemba in 1897.

These overlapping phases of Zanzibar's history had a crucial and lasting impact on the islands. The history of slavery meant that everyone was seen, and many categorized themselves, as either 'Arabs', or associates of 'Arabs', and ex- slave owners and therefore Mabwana (privileged masters); or as African ex-slaves and victims of the Mabwana. Despite these tensions, however, in the years before British colonialism full-blown racial conflict did not occur.

These divisions do not coincide with inequalities or hierarchies in Zanzibari society either today or half a century ago. Then as now a large majority of the population was of mixed Arab and African heritage, and the categories of Arab and African were so fluid that between 1924 and 1948 the percentage of those identifying as Arabs had risen from 8.7 per cent to 16.9 per cent mainly because many non-Arabs had 'decided to 'join' the Arab community' (Lofchie, 1965: 74), with no questions asked or impediments created.

But unfortunately the fears and anxieties of that history of colonialism and slavery have continued to haunt the Isles and have been whipped up time and again by unscrupulous politicians.

In the mid-20th century, the islands were not formally a colony but a British protectorate. But protectorates were hardly different from colonies in terms of exploitation – the Sultan was a constitutional monarch on a salary from the British, and it was they who controlled the government, the markets and the trade routes, and pocketed the profits from Zanzibar's famous products – cloves and coconuts.

The class and ethnic divisions in the rural population of the two islands of Zanzibar were at the time somewhat different, and also of course different from what they are today. In Unguja, there were absentee small landowners who lived mainly in the town, subsistence farmers on less fertile ground, and squatters on the plantations. In the 1950s, these landlords in Unguja were almost all Arabs. The subsistence farmers in Unguja were mainly Shirazis, a group who had intermingled like everyone else in Zanzibar but traced their ancestry to Shiraz in Iran, from where migration to Zanzibar had occurred as far back as the 10th century. The squatters were people who had come originally as contract labourers from mainland Tanganyika in the clove-picking seasons but had stayed on and established roots locally through marriage, and had, over the generations, become completely integrated into Zanzibari society.

Zanzibar town, on the western tip of Unguja, was a highly

sophisticated city which although ancient was also modern – it had electric street lighting well before London did. It was populated by merchants, traders, street vendors, shopkeepers, casual labourers, dockworkers, transport workers and so on.

However, ethnicity and class did not coincide, and nor was the class structure entirely rigid. For example, although Shirazis formed the majority of subsistence peasants and Africans (who were often migrants from the mainland) formed the majority of urban workers, these ethnic groups, like others, were spread across class divisions (Kuper, 1970: 366).

Pemba, in contrast to Unjuga, was almost entirely rural in the 1950s and less technologically developed. Here the land was rich and fertile, and there were fewer large landowners and a larger proportion of Shirazi and Arab middle and rich peasants.[2]

The way colonial capitalism developed meant that various ethnic groups found themselves drawn into, and sometimes confined to, specific occupations and economic positions which were often in conflict with each other. For example, South Asians who had arrived in Zanzibar as early as the 1st century AD as traders and merchants (Bader, 1991: 170) found their economic activities circumscribed in the last quarter of the 19th century. Partly as a result, a significant proportion of better-off South Asians turned to money-lending. In the process they impoverished the Arab landowners who were vulnerable to the fluctuations in the price of cloves, and this inevitably led to tensions between the two groups.

As in other colonies, in Zanzibar, British colonial policy also intensified and shaped existing racial tensions. Against a background of racist colonial ideology, which saw Arabs through an orientalist lens as dissolute, conspicuous consumers with large numbers of children (Lofchie, 1965: 108) and at the same time regarded Africans as fit only to be an underclass, the colonial administration set up racially identified associations to which every citizen was required to belong. There were as many as 23 such associations – the African Association, the Arab Association (subdivided further into Omani, Hadhramout and Yemeni Associations), the Shirazi Association and so on. These associations, which were led by the dominant classes within each group, institutionalized racial divisions and engendered racial antagonism.

At the same time the education system set up by the British perpetuated class and racial inequalities, since with a few exceptions it provided state-assisted education effectively only to the sons of privileged classes (Sheriff, 1991: 87).

As the reports and letters of the period show, British colonial racism meant that as in other parts of the empire, people were labelled, and thought of by the British, only in terms of their ethnic and religious identity. There was an unwillingness to acknowledge that different groups and individuals had any political identity. The only exception to this rule was where people were suspected of being 'communists', and therefore dominated by foreign masters, Chinese or Russian, confirming the underlying assumption that these colonized people were not capable of thinking for themselves. The Americans who were to play such a profound role in the shaping of Zanzibar and Tanganyika's future adopted an identical perspective.

Anti-Colonial Struggle and the First Nationalist Party

The early 1950s saw an upsurge of nationalist consciousness in Zanzibar. The colonial Legislative Council had consisted, before 1946, of Europeans, Arabs and Indians, and even after 1946 African representation was kept small. The British had made it clear that this was unlikely to change in the foreseeable future. 'Institutionalization of full parliamentary democracy was viewed as an extremely long-range enterprise in political tutelage...The notion that democratic self-government could occur only after many generations of careful instruction characterized British attitudes in many colonies' (Lofchie, 1965: 19).

Given the racially stratified nature of Zanzibari society, one of the few ways people could make their voices heard was through the newspapers of their associations. The more radical members of the Arab Association, for example, now began to use the association's paper *Al Falaq* to oppose the policy of communal representation in the Legislative Council.[3]

If anti-colonial consciousness was growing, one of the early struggles against colonialism was a peasant uprising which took place between 1951 and 1954 in the west of Unguja not far from Zanzibar town. The British crushed it brutally.

The revolt had two immediate causes. The first was the appropriation by the colonial government of large tracts of land belonging mainly to middle peasant households – in other words families who worked on their own land, and did not hire in, or hire out, agricultural labour – to build an airport; and the second was the forced inoculation of cattle against anthrax and compulsory dipping against East Coast fever. The compulsory dipping had been introduced in 1948: not only did the peasants have to pay for it but it had resulted in a number of cows dying. (As the officials later acknowledged, dipping a cow could lead to its losing its immunity against disease, causing it to catch infections and die if regular dipping was not continued.)

Cattle were an important source of income for the peasants, and when the government tried to introduce compulsory inoculation the peasants refused. Arrests and fines led to a boycott of various administration activities. Nineteen peasant leaders were convicted but when they were being driven away to prison, peasants from nearby areas who had surrounded the court ambushed the van and released eleven of them. They then tried to storm the prison to try to release the others. The police fired on them, killing nine people (Bowles, 1991: 95).

The crushing of the uprising led to the setting-up of the first political movement for independence the Party of National Unity for the Sultan's Subjects (PNUSS) by the peasants – the name reflecting the party's aim of uniting groups with differing ethnicities and at the same time including not only people of Unguja and Pemba but the Swahili-speaking people of the Kenyan coast. The identity 'Sultan's subjects' must be understood against a background where the Sultan was not regarded as a foreign power, unlike the British. In fact there were stories told by peasants in Zanzibar about how their forefathers had travelled to Oman to seek the assistance of the Sultan against Portuguese colonialism (Babu, 1991: 223).

News of the revolt and the repression it had unleashed spread through the urban and rural areas of Zanzibar like wildfire. The colonial government reacted with panic. They feared the spirit of the Mau Mau rebellion was spreading, and not just among the peasants but to other sections of society.

They also clearly feared Arab-African unity, and threatened to enforce a law which made political activity by civil servants illegal. This effectively blocked African civil servants from political involvement, and affected the politics of the African Association enormously. The president of the African Association had been a progressive government doctor, he now had to withdraw from politics, and Abeid Karume, a former seaman and later a boat owner and head of the Boat

Owners Federation, became its president. The African Association under Karume began to take a conservative and anti-Arab position – opposing what it saw as Arab nationalism, at the same time as it began to campaign for communal representation to continue, no matter that it disempowered Africans (Lofchie, 1965: 166).

When articles in *Al Falaq* expressed their solidarity with the peasant uprising and condemned the violence of the colonial response, the British responded by charging its publisher and the entire executive committee of the Arab Association with sedition. Among these committee members was Ali Muhsin, later one of the central figures of the nationalist movement. The Arab Association withdrew all their representatives from the Legislative Council, condemning it as communal and demanding immediate progress towards self-government. This boycott was completely effective for a year and a half.

The sedition trial had an enormous impact on people's political consciousness across the country. Urban workers, craftspeople, the petty bourgeoisie and intellectuals began to join the PNUSS. The peasants who were the party's founders welcomed them in, because it meant the party now possessed the skills that the peasants themselves could not provide. Soon the PNUSS began to evolve into a fully fledged nationalist party. It changed its name and in 1955 became the Zanzibar Nationalist Party (ZNP). Ali Muhsin became its leader.

The party began to campaign for non-racial representation in the Legislative Council, the right for all adults to vote and a new constitution committing the government to early independence.

British Fears and the Formation of the Afro-Shirazi Party

The British felt deeply threatened by this situation. As documents of the period show, in private they expressed their fears about the emergence of the ZNP as a liberation movement, and in line with cold war thinking, they assumed that the party was packed full of communists who were in the pay of the Soviet Union and China. Publicly however, they projected the ZNP-led anti-colonial movement as a development which the people of Zanzibar should fear.

To the Arab landowners they depicted the movement as a direct threat to their personal privilege and to their position in the economy. To the African and Shirazi petty bourgeoisie they presented the movement as a skilful Arab 'front' organization designed to get rid of the British and expose the masses of Africans to the mercy of the Arabs (Babu, 1991: 225).

In line with this construction, British diplomats busied themselves trying to encourage the formation of an African party which would oppose the ZNP and be loyal to the British. This was made easier by the nature of the existing African Association, which was not in any way anti-colonial, and had in fact urged the 1956 Coutts Constitutional Commission to retain communal representatives in the Legislative Council for at least five years.

The British schemes however floundered for a while because the African Association had few allies. Pemba Shirazis, who were mainly rich peasants, led by individuals like retired schoolmaster Mohammed Shamte and landowner Ali Shariff, did not want to ally with it. The reason they gave was that they did not want to be part of something so inherently racist in its approach. But behind this was a narrow, essentially right-wing Shirazi nationalism based on an anti-African and anti-Arab hostility.

However, help was at hand for the British because at this stage Julius Nyerere, then leader of the Tanganyika African National Union (TANU), chose to intervene: not to forge unity between the ZNP and the African Association, as might have been expected, but to create a unified front against what he clearly regarded as an Arab party. He visited Zanzibar several times in 1956 to persuade Africans and Shirazis to create such a front against the Arabs (Lofchie, 1965: 1668). In hindsight this was perhaps an early indication of the role he was to play after the revolution.

Eventually in February 1957, shortly before the election, an alliance called the Afro-Shirazi Union (ASU) was set up, with the African Association and the Shirazi Association in Unguja agreeing to cooperate during the forthcoming elections (but not to merge) and the Shirazi Association of Pemba refusing to do so (Sheriff, 1991: 134).

The ZNP reacted to the formation of the ASU by accusing its leader Karume of not being an 'authentic' Zanzibari citizen and taking him to court. This absurd accusation, and the narrow nationalism it displayed, turned Karume into a martyr. He easily won the case, and the verdict, coming just before the election, meant that the sympathy vote swept him to recognition as a 'national leader'.

The election led to a decisive defeat for the ZNP. However the ASU did not win the elections either, receiving less than two-fifths of the total vote in the islands and three of the six elected seats in the Legislative Council. A few months later the Pemba Shirazis reluctantly agreed to cooperate with the ASU, and the Afro-Shirazi Party was formed.

Karume's party's slogan during the election campaign – '*Uhuru Zuia*' (stop the move to independence) – made the position of the ASP as allies of the British quite clear. Karume, despite his fear and hatred of Arabs, remained capable of startlingly servile behaviour. Subsequent to a speech he had made which he felt in retrospect might offend the Sultan, Karume wrote to him on July 26, 1958 as follows:

> Your Highness, I am your subject and along with all the members of the ASP I wish to pledge before you my sincere loyalty to you. I myself, Abeid Amani Karume wish to bring before you the truth, my Sultan. During my speech in Raha Leo, I thought I used some civilized words, but I did not know the meaning of these. Therefore it is my intention and the intention of my colleagues, from the bottom of our hearts, our beloved King Maulana, to beg and make it known to you that we are under your feet and under your Sultanate. We are obedient, without hesitation, to your every order. We all know your sincere goodness and generosity. I beg you to forgive my mistakes for using language which I did not understand, Maulana. I am under your feet and remain obedient. Abeid Amaani Karume.
>
> (National Archives Zanzibar, July 1958)

Was the letter written on British orders? Or was it Karume's own idea? It may well have been the former, because Karume was very much the grateful and obedient British subject. He is known to have commented, while arguing for a continuation of British colonial rule, 'We will learn something from the British; the Arabs are backward just like us' (Ayani, 1970: 50). Either way it provides an insight into the man who was soon to rule Zanzibar.

The ASP's class character at this point must be regarded as petty bourgeois. By 1957, its leader Karume was no longer a merchant seaman but a motorboat owner, and its support 'was clearly among the relatively well-off section of the Zanzibar population (excluding the landowners)' (Bowles, 1991: 100).

Revolutionary Sparks in the Air of Zanzibar

It was in this period that Abdulrahman Mohamed Babu returned to Zanzibar after six years in London. His father, who came from a family of Islamic scholars, was of mixed Swahili and Comoro descent. His mother, who was from a mercantile Arab family, though she had an Oromo grandmother, had died when he was two years old, and he had been brought up by a great-aunt who had a house in Stone Town in Unguja. She was, Babu often reminisced, 'a strong woman – a fighter' who never attempted to force him to conform to convention.

After his schooling, Babu worked as a 'weighing clerk' in the Clove Growers' Association and saved money to go to England for further studies. London in the 1950s was full of radicalism, progressive causes and anti-colonial movements, so although he had planned to study accountancy, this soon changed. While he worked to make ends meet, he studied philosophy and English literature, was drawn first to anarchism and then to Marxism, and became involved in anti-colonial politics. He was, for example, the secretary of the East and Central Africa Committee of the influential Movement for Colonial Freedom and, together with Samir Amin and Frene Jinwallah, a co-editor of the Paris-based magazine *Africa Latin America Asia – Revolution*.

He was also increasingly involved in the politics of Pan-Africanism. In this historic era of liberation struggles and revolutionary victories, one of the most significant political influences on Africans of Babu's generation was Nkrumah's victory in Ghana. As he wrote:

> Coming as it did after the Chinese Revolution, the Viet Minh victory against the French at Dien Bien Phu(1954) and the Algerian Revolution... Ghana's victory introduced us in a concrete way to the importance and effectiveness of the 'mass political party' against colonialism.
>
> (Babu, 1996: 325)

However he was also, like many other young Africans and Asians of the period, inspired by the Chinese revolution. He had studied it in detail, but particularly for its relevance to Africa. China's socialist revolution, he wrote:

> was an extension of its own liberation struggle and consequently there was a very thin dividing line between her nationalism and socialism. This dual loyalty to the two great movements of the period, enabled the Chinese to share more intimately the sentiments and aspirations of Africa's liberation struggles and the struggle for national reconstruction both of which were Africa's top priority.
>
> (Babu, [1987a] 2002: 166)

Babu soon after his return from London in 1957
Source: Mohamed Amin/Camerapix.

Towards the end of his time in London, the ZNP leadership had arranged for Babu to be trained in party organization by the British Labour Party, and soon after he returned to Zanzibar he was made the general secretary of the ZNP.[4]

In the years after the 1957 election and the ZNP's disastrous defeat, he set about reorganizing and rebuilding the party, with tireless energy and an infectious optimism. A strong network of branches was established all over the country, and regular weekly meetings began to be held at local level, attended by a representative of the national executive. This allowed the party to involve the people and reflect their needs and experiences while maintaining unity, while at the same time giving local leaders a strong sense of the party as a national organization with national objectives, and discouraging regional rivalries and jealousies.

Babu's aim was to build the ZNP into a mass party which unified the entire country in a struggle against colonialism. He sought to bring people from all racial groupings and classes together on an ideological anti-colonial basis, but also to highlight the reality of class differences within racial groups and the need to unite the working class and poor peasants.

To this end he set up the ZNPs first youth organization, the Youths Own Union (YOU), to reach out to primary and secondary-school children and to urban and rural youth, male and female, of all classes and races. It became enormously popular, providing a new vitality to the party and also making the question of unity central both ideologically and in terms of practical work. Its success was a testimony to Babu's ability to translate theory into organizational practice, and to perceive and encourage the best in others. He is remembered by his comrades as in many ways an exemplary revolutionary leader – incorruptible and principled but never dogmatic, charismatic and confident but never arrogant, committed and serious but warm, accessible and ready to see the funny side of things.

Shaaban Salim and Hamed Hilal were students when they first got involved with the ZNP, Hamed in 1958 and Shaaban in 1960. They had their formative political education through the YOU. Shaaban recounted those exciting days. 'We grew up within the YOU, with lectures and debates. We began for the first time to consciously think about colonialism and imperialism and how we could fight them' (interview with Shaaban Salim, 2009). It was the formation of YOU, according to Hamed Hilal, which transformed the ZNP into a powerful political force.

There were debating forums dealing with specific issues to bring out the real meaning of ideological struggle, there were drama and education forums, a thoroughgoing literacy campaign across Zanzibar. There were mobilizations demanding secondary education for all and against racial policies, and demonstrations in support of liberation

Schoolgirl members of YOU photographed by the British anxious about 'militant youth'
Source: Public Record Office CO 822/1377.

of Algeria and Palestine and against the apartheid regime of South Africa.

These activities were like revolutionary sparks in the air of Zanzibar – transforming the political scene, raising the consciousness of young people, renewing that faith in themselves which colonialism seeks deliberately to erode, and making them aware that their own future and that of their country was in their own hands.

This confidence and commitment began to be openly expressed as, for example, in this conference resolution by the All Zanzibar Students Association which was reported in *ZaNews*, the paper founded by Babu which was the voice of the left in Zanzibar: 'We have a great role to play in present developments that are unfolding in our country. We have always been at the forefront of our people's struggles against colonialism and imperialism' (i, 1963). *ZaNews* was at the time one of the very few newspapers in East Africa that regularly reported on national and international anti-imperialist and working-class struggles.

YOU activities were watched carefully and fearfully by the British. They spied on the YOU, even collecting photographs of schoolchildren marching and members relaxing on picnics. And in an uncanny parallel with the paranoia generated by the 'war on terror', they were worried by the apparent militancy of YOU members.

As for Babu, the colonialists became increasingly anxious about his growing popularity and organizing powers, and what the British Resident, the most senior colonial post in a protectorate, called his 'hold over the frustrated, unemployed youth of the ZNP' (Public Record Office, 1962a).

He was, in fact, far from alone politically. The ZNP had attracted a number of other talented young men – socialists as well as progressive nationalists. They included Ali Sultan Issa, Khamis Ameir, Abu Bakar, Quallatein Badawi, Hamed Hilal, Shaaban Salim, Muhsin Abeid, Aburazak Mussa Simai, Amar Salim (Kuku), Ali Khatib Chwaya, Mohamed Abdulla Baramia, Kadiria Mnyeji, and Salim Rashid and Salim Ahmed Salim, who were both at separate times general secretaries of YOU. It was the collective work, creative energy and enthusiasm of all these men – who were later to become Umma Party members – that helped reverse the fortunes of the ZNP in this period.[5]

A few of them, like Babu, had returned from Britain in the mid-1950s. Ali Sultan Issa, for example, had left Zanzibar at the age of 18 as a stowaway and seaman on ships travelling across the world. He had arrived in London after a journey during which he spent months stopping over in Calcutta, Cape Town and Vancouver. He too had been drawn to anti-colonial political circles in London and had eventually joined the British Communist Party before returning to Zanzibar, joining the ZNP, and becoming its international representative.

Quallatein Badawi, an inspired trade union leader, had been active in the Zanzibar Club set up by graduates from Makerere and London universities, many of whom too had links with the British Communist Party. Later he and Khamis Ameir were central to the ZNP's trade union work.

When Badawi passed away in November 2011, his comrade and friend Salim Msoma wrote a poignant tribute to him (Msoma, 2011). He described how in the 1950s and 1960s Zanzibaris who landed in Britain as seamen were often drawn to the Communist movement: 'every single one of them was received by Badawi when they returned to Zanzibar. He made sure he was at the baggage room of the docks or at the airport to embrace them.'

Khamis Ameir, now in his 80s, still lives in Zanzibar. Like Babu, he too had studied and worked in London. On his journey back to Zanzibar, he had stopped over in Nairobi and come across Ali Sultan, who was on his way to Cairo to set up an office for the ZNP. Khamis told me:

I remember the intense discussions we had all night. When I came back to Zanzibar, I was eager to begin political work. I met Badawi who had worked as a customs officer and had joined the Zanzibar and Pemba Federation of Trade Unions (ZPFTU) which was affiliated to the ASP. Badawi was not happy with the ZPFTU partly because like the ASP it was demanding that independence be delayed and partly because it was affiliated to the ICFTU. The ICFTU was the trade union federation set up by the US during the Cold War era to control and subdue anti-imperialist trade unions in Third World countries.

(interview with Khamis Ameir, 2009)

Badawi suggested that Khamis join the ZNP and work with its trade union, which is what he did. He was involved in organizing rural workers and seafaring workers, who were mainly dhow crews, in the Maritime and Allied Workers Union, of which he became the general secretary. The ZNP, he told me, was also involved at that time organizing metal workers, workers in the small factories making soap and others. The unions not only actively supported the workers, representing them in demanding better wages and conditions, but also provided political education.

By 1960 Badawi left the ZPFTU and he and Khamis worked to unite the two unions which supported ZNP – the Agricultural and Allied Workers Union and the Maritime and Allied Workers Union – to form the Federation of Progressive Trade Unions (FPTU). 1960 saw strikes in a number of industries over wages and working conditions, and the next year dhow crews went on strike for 84 days – the longest in Zanzibar's history. The strike was wholly successful, ending with all the workers' demands being met (Hadjivayanis and Ferguson, 1991: 209).

The FPTU had two newspapers which came out regularly in the early 1960s, a Swahili daily, *Kibarua*, and an English weekly, *Worker*. Both papers defended the workers' immediate interests while at the same time putting across a line which was anti-colonial and against US imperialism. Badawi worked in the international department of the FPTU forging links with other progressive trade unions abroad (interview with Khamis Ameir, 2009).

Outside the trade union movement too, the ZNP built a wide network of alliances and developed a clear Pan-African and anti-imperialist perspective, supporting the Mau Mau movement in Kenya, TANU in Tanganyika, the struggle against the Central African Federation, the Algerian revolution, and the anti-apartheid and liberation movements in Southern Africa. Its anti-imperialist perspective led it also to make links with the Palestinian struggle and to support China's rightful admission to the United Nations.

Meanwhile, the United States was increasingly dismayed by the party's popularity. It began to condemn it as an 'Arab party' and at the same time began to keep a careful eye on developments in Zanzibar. To this end US officials tried to establish close relationships with ZNP and ASP leaders they could influence, funded frequent visits from the CIA's trade union man, Irving Brown, in an attempt to draw Zanzibari trade union leaders into the ICFTU, and set up a NASA 'tracking station' – the *Mercury* despite strong opposition from the ZNP.

Through the *Mercury*, NASA could keep an eye not only on the islands but on the western Indian Ocean and East Africa as a whole. This was clearly a predecessor of the US 'presence' in the Indian Ocean today. In addition the Americans began to set up a network of stooges and informers in Zanzibar itself (Wilson, 1989: 11).

As for the British, the comments of the senior civil servant P. A. P. Robertson provide a glimpse of their underlying desperation at this stage. Babu, Robertson recollected in a recorded interview in 1971, was not only 'a thorn in the flesh' of the government but 'the most sinister man in Zanzibar ... an evil genius' (cited by Smith, 1971).

Racial Tensions: The Pan African Movement Intervenes

There had always been political differences within the ZNP between the right and left wings, but unity had been carefully nurtured by the party's tight-knit but democratic structure, which Babu and others on the left had worked hard to build. In the late 1950s, however, contradictions within the ZNP began to intensify. This perhaps was not surprising given the range of class interests and groups that had been drawn to the party. A sizeable section of the right wing were still loyal to the Sultan and also put the interests of landowners first, while the left sought to draw peasants, workers and squatters into the ZNP and represent their interests so that the party could speak for the country as a whole.

The ASP also had by now a variety of class interests within it – workers, peasants, some landowners (though a smaller number than those in the ZNP) and also merchants and big-business representatives from the Indian National Association, whose views became enormously influential within the party. It had however a very limited number of intellectuals, and began to rely more and more on TANU intellectuals for political analysis. This dependence on the mainland exacerbated the existing tensions within the party between Karume and his supporters and the Pemba Shirazis.

At the same time the ASP started to foment racial hatred. The first nine months of 1958 were fraught with racial tension. ASP cadres began to target Arab supporters of the ZNP, organizing boycotts of shops in rural areas, which forced hundreds of Arab shopkeepers out of business, and threatening Arab small landowners. Arab landowners responded by evicting the squatters on their land.

Finally in September 1958, the issue of Arab–African tension in Zanzibar and the related issue of conflict between the two main parties were discussed in a Pan-African context. The Pan African Freedom Movement of East and Central Africa (PAFMECA) was holding its inaugural meeting in Mwanza, Tanganyika. Delegates from both the ZNP and ASP attended. The violence in Zanzibar between supporters of the two parties was among the issues discussed. The ZNP presented its aims of trying to build a multi-racial anti-colonial movement, while the ASP presented its position as wishing to delay independence because it felt the country was not ready. Eventually, after a long period of discussion, a directive was issued by PAFMECA that when more than one party in a country was a member of PAFMECA, they should collaborate in a Freedom Committee consisting of the leaders from both parties. This, it was felt, would prevent internal divisions which inevitably played into the hands of the colonialists.

The establishment of the Freedom Committee brought a period of harmony between the ZNP and ASP, demonstrating that earlier political leaders had played a crucial role in fomenting racial tension. Leaders of the two parties toured the country together, condemned acts of racial aggression and spoke of the importance of unity and their determination to establish 'a joint nationalist front for Zanzibar' (Lofchie, 1965: 191). Boycotts and evictions ceased, and racial tensions eased almost immediately.

This was a time when the Pan-African Movement was growing stronger – ushering in an inspiring period of solidarity and alliance between various anti-colonial struggles in Africa. In December 1958, the first All African People's Conference (AAPC) was held in Accra, Ghana.

In the outline to the memoirs which he never found time to write, Babu provides us with a glimpse of that exciting time. The Zanzibari delegation stopped over in Leopoldville in what was then the Belgian Congo on its way to Accra. In this city overshadowed by Belgian colonialism, they had a remarkable chance encounter with Patrice Lumumba. On enquiring discreetly among the workers at their hotel about political movements in the country, they found their way late at night to a nightclub in the African section of the racially segregated colonial city. There they came across Lumumba and his comrades, who till then, because of the machinations of the Belgians, had been completely isolated from all Pan-African movements and alliances (Babu, [1987b] 2002: 64).

Attending the AAPC was an unforgettable experience for the ZNP leftists, as Babu was to write:

> Meeting Nkrumah for the first time was a most exhilarating experience …. This opened the way to meeting Sekou Toure, the African hero of the time, fresh from voting 'no' to French arrogance and domination of West Africa. Frantz Fanon was at his best and succeeded in changing the theme of the AAPC Conference from 'non-violent' liberation struggle to struggle 'by any means'. Dr Moumie of UPC Cameroon ably chaired the political committee of the AAPC which devised an Africa-wide strategy for liberation and unity among liberation movements.
> (Babu, 1996: 326)

Typically in this description Babu fails to mention his own contribution. Eminent scholar and lawyer Bereket Habte Selassie had these memories of him at the AAPC:

> To young Africans like myself at the time, it was a moment at once defining and awe-inspiring. Babu came as the head of a Zanzibari progressive political party. He and Lumumba struck those of us who were young and inexperienced with their humility and attentiveness to our views as well as the vigour with which they put forward their views and shared their knowledge. This spirit of humility, combined with dedication and commitment … won him the love and admiration of young Africans.
> (Habte Selassie, 1996: 333)

During the conference Kwame Nkrumah and George Padmore organized a special meeting at Nkrumah's residence to strengthen the unity between the ASP and ZNP. It was attended by Ali Muhsin and

Karume, representing the ZNP and ASP respectively, by Babu as the secretary of the Freedom Committee, and Kanyama Chiume of the Malawi Congress Party as the official representative of PAFMECA.

At this meeting Karume voiced his concerns about the possibility of a split in his party because the Pemba branch led by Mohamed Shamte had already expressed their antipathy to working with the ZNP. At the end of the meeting Ali Muhsin and Karume signed the so-called Accra Accord. In it they pledged to support the ASP/ZNP united front and never to support any splinter group from either party – if splits occurred as a result of the implementation of the Accord or the Freedom Committee.

An Opportunistic Alliance of the Right

However less than a year after the signing of the Accra Accord, sections of the ASP became reluctant to continue its participation in the Freedom Committee.

In mid-April PAFMECA held a conference in Zanzibar in which the Pan-African leaders urged unity. At this conference Nyerere, who had only a few years earlier encouraged the formation of the ASP as a party in opposition to the ZNP, now criticized Zanzibaris for not working together towards independence. He told the meeting 'the atmosphere

Accra, All African People's Conference 1958. Left to right, Kanyama Chiume, Malawi; Joshua Nkomo, Zimbabwe; Hastings Banda, Malawi; Kenneth Kaunda, Zambia; Abdulrahman Mohamed Babu, Zanzibar.

of masters and slaves still exists in Zanzibar ... politically the parties all agree to one objective but they opposed each other because of race' (Lofchie, 1965: 191). This remarkable U-turn can only be ascribed to a realization on his part that the ASP (which was dominated by TANU) would not be able to take Zanzibar to independence on its own, and that therefore at this point unity with the ZNP must be encouraged. Despite these interventions, however, those in the ASP who had been opposed to working with the ZNP did not change their approach.

In June 1959, there was another attempt to convince these dissidents. As the British Intelligence Report for the month of June 1959 reveals, a secret conference was called by Karume in Zanzibar at which Rashidi Kawawa, then a Central Committee Member of TANU, was present. On the first three days little headway was made, with Pemba delegates Othman Shariff, Mohamed Shamte, Ali Shariff and others 'doubting the necessity of co-operating with the Nationalists' (Public Record Office, 1959: 6). Then on June 28, as the British document continues:

> Abeid Karume produced to the meeting a document signed by Julius Nyerere and purporting to be a statement of TANU policy. It is said to have been agreed to by PAFMECA delegates of Kenya, Uganda and the Central African Federation. ... The document stated:
> a) That the Afro-Shirazi community had no need to fear the results of cooperating with the Nationalists in the achievement of independence because it was recognized by all that the Afro-Shirazis were the rightful owners of Zanzibar;
> b) That the Afro-Shirazi community had no need to fear the consequence of early independence for educational reasons because TANU would see that Zanzibari educated Africans working in Tanganyika Government Departments were made available to the Afro-Shirazi Party when independence was achieved;
> c) That eventually, on the achievement of independence of Tanganyika and Zanzibar, the two territories would be joined together in one African Republic;
> d) That the Afro-Shirazi Party must recognize that other communities who were Zanzibaris had political rights;
> The document ended by requesting the signatures of Abeid Karume and Othman Shariff if the policy was acceptable and both signed.
> This assurance of TANU completely dispelled any fears which existed concerning the political aspirations of the Afro-Shirazi community and it was agreed that ... the discussions of the past few days, including the TANU document would be kept a close secret.
> (Public Record Office, 1959: 6–7)

The document had the desired effect: all members of the executive committee of the ASP, including Othman Shariff and Mohamed Shamte, took an oath not to destroy the unity of the ASP.

Although the Pemba delegates broke their oath soon after this, the meeting was still one of crucial importance. It effectively gave Nyerere's stamp of approval to the notion that the Afro-Shirazis (and no other group) were the 'rightful owners of Zanzibar', and confirmed his cooperation in the ultimate aim – that 'on the achievement of independence of Tanganyika and Zanzibar, the two territories would be joined together in one African Republic'. The British appear to have been complicit in the whole process.

By late 1959, ASP supporters again began to attack Arabs, and at the same time the right wing of the ZNP, which had always been opposed to the Freedom Committee, began to foment racial tension. Many of the landowners in the ZNP began to evict the squatters on their land in a second round of racial violence.

Within a few months, in December 1959, the split that Karume had feared did occur. The Pemba section of the party, dominated by the most influential Shirazis – rich peasants, merchants, shopkeepers and bus owners, and under the leadership of Mohamed Shamte, who was one of those most virulently opposed to working with Arabs, left the ASP and formed a new party – the Zanzibar and Pemba People's Party (ZPPP).

At this point the ZNP right wing revealed their true nature, broke the Accra Accord and turned enthusiastically to the ZPPP to engineer an alliance. Shamte cynically abandoned his earlier position and accepted this offer.

The split in the ASP had occurred at the worst possible time for the left. The Freedom Committee was in recess and Babu, its secretary, was away in Cairo, negotiating the setting up of a ZNP mission. He was also scheduled to go to China on an official visit to meet the top leadership of the Chinese Communist Party, a trip he could not cancel. As he wrote later, he was shocked by the duplicity of the ZNP leadership:

> Our painstaking work for the unity of the people of Zanzibar was suddenly in ruin, as if this was not bad enough, more shocking news came from my own party, that the ZNP warmly welcomed the split and that our leaders were actively collaborating with ZPPP leaders in opposition to the ASP ....We were witnessing the end of our carefully

nurtured inter-party unity. It was victory for the reactionaries in both parties and goodbye to Zanzibar's political stability.

(Babu, 1995: 5)

This crucial period in Zanzibar's history was shaped by a number of factors, but particularly by the change in membership of the parties. With the country on the brink of an election to be followed by internal self-government, the membership of both parties and particularly the ZNP had increased. These new members of the ZNP were often civil servants who now saw their careers in politics. Their presence enormously strengthened the right wing of the party. Deeply anti-communist after their years in the colonial civil service, and concerned about the influence of the mainland, in case this robbed them of the jobs they sought, they saw the alliance with the ZPPP as their opportunity for electoral victory which would lead to key positions in government.

As for the ZPPP, its leadership was largely rich peasants and intellectuals from Pemba (who felt they had been neglected because of the influence of mainland intellectuals in the ASP). Zanzibar now witnessed the remarkable spectacle of erstwhile ASP leaders who had been driven by their hatred and fear of Arabs eagerly allying with those they had shunned, all in the interests of personal gain.

With the exit of Pemba intellectuals, the ASP was left with no Zanzibari intellectuals at all, and possibly as a result the leadership turned increasingly to TANU and also the Indian National Association (particularly the wealthy Indian merchants from Pemba who became a dominating influence on the party) for support and advice.

Strategies of the Left in a Reactionary Climate

In this situation of discord and constant hostility from the right wing of the party and the colonial government, the left wing considered a number of possible strategies. Given their view of colonialism as the primary contradiction, they did not regard the struggle against the ASP as primary, particularly since it had now agreed to participate fully in the independence struggle. This made some of them feel it might be worth collectively joining the ASP. But the majority felt that they should remain in the ZNP, which they themselves had worked so hard to create and had struggled so much to put back on a revolutionary course.

ANTI-COLONIAL STRUGGLES

The ideological struggle in this period was based on a Marxist analysis of the class structure, but this analysis did not come from textbooks. It was the result of a dialectical relationship between theory and practical experience. For example, in relation to the difficulty of organizing urban workers with strong links to the mainland, Babu noted that their class solidarity with other workers was uncertain and difficult to develop. They had, for example, acted as scabs in confrontations between local workers and employers. 'Their support of the ASP was primarily for self-preservation, and their nationalism was racial rather than political. They were loyal primarily to TANU and only incidentally to the ASP' (Babu, 1991: 234). The left, while not identifying with them wholly, had to show them the essential similarity between the working-class struggle in Zanzibar and the mainland, the differences being only a result of different conditions in Zanzibar. In other words, they had to educate them on the theory and practice of class struggle.

As for the indigenous workers, faced with the threat of losing their jobs to mainland workers, they had developed an extreme antipathy towards them, and therefore they were vulnerable to the right-wing and anti-mainlander propaganda of the ZNP and ZPPP. This would intensify the already explosive racial animosities, playing into the hands of the colonialists.

There was also the peasant base of the ZNP, the people who had laid its foundations. Not all of them were aware of the conflict within the party, and the left faced a dilemma. Bringing the conflict formally to their notice might have weakened the party and played into the hands of the colonialists. On the other hand, when the revolutionary struggle intensified, it was important that they should not be taken by surprise.

These were the ideological struggles with which the left found themselves grappling. Should they have resigned from the ZNP and formed a new party at this point? Was it not an error to stay on in the ZNP at this stage?

While it may be tempting to think so in hindsight, and speculate that if the Umma Party had been launched at this stage it would have had time to consolidate for a few more months prior to independence, and Zanzibari politics would have been very different, the political realities of the era do not suggest that this would have been possible.

Under colonial rule, particularly during the cold war, the scale of repression against the left made it extremely difficult, almost impossible, for a left party to exist. Leftist individuals had to be active within existing nationalist anti-colonial movements and demonstrate through their own approach, honesty and commitment the distinctive qualities of such a leadership. This laid the foundation for a future Marxist leadership. This is why leaving the ZNP and launching the Umma Party was no easy decision, and why the left did not take it at this stage. Babu reflected on some of the issues underlying these decisions in a letter to Karim Essack (see Babu, [1982a] 2002).

The activities of the left were also made increasingly difficult by the rapid deterioration of what little racial harmony there still was. Soon after the split the ASP began another campaign of racism against Arabs, and the right wing of the ZNP, which was now increasingly vocal, responded with anti-African speeches, while the ZPPP began to spread propaganda against mainlanders.

CHAPTER TWO

The British Transfer Power to the Sultan and His Allies

The British, the ZNP–ZPPP Alliance, and Dirty Tricks

The leaders of the new ZNP–ZPPP alliance now moved further to the right and closer to the Sultan than the ZNP on its own had ever been. The next election was held in January 1961, and the period leading up to it was one of intense racial campaigning by both the ASP and the ZNP–ZPPP alliance.

The elections results proved indecisive, the 22 elected representatives being split equally between the two contenders. Since neither had a parliamentary majority, an interim caretaker government was set up and another election was held in June that year. The British, eager for the right-wing ZNP–ZPPP combination to gain control, created a new parliamentary constituency in South Pemba to avoid any possibility of another deadlock, and the next election in June 1961 delivered the victory they desired. It was, however, accompanied and followed by riots in Zanzibar town and rural areas which the government was unable to control. Some 60 to 100 people including many women and children, most of them from Arab shop-owning families, lost their lives and nearly 400 were injured. The British imposed a State of Emergency and brought in troops to patrol the islands for the next 20 months (Lofchie, 1965: 212).

Even at this stage, however, the parties did not agree. The ASP demanded, first, that self-government be delayed, and second, that another election be held before any changes occurred. There appeared to be total deadlock.

Hamed Hilal remembered that period. He was going to England for further studies and since he did not have enough money for the boat fare, he went by land. He travelled via Dar es Salaam, Mombasa, Nairobi, Kampala, Jumba in southern Sudan, Asyut in Egypt and then to Cairo. Here, however, his trip to London was interrupted because Ali Sultan was in Cairo working at the ZNP office and he asked Hamed to stay at his house and help him with some work. 'Then other comrades arrived', he told me. 'Shaaban Salim, Ahmada Shafi and Abdulla Juma, they all came through the mainland. After the 1961 January election some of us received military training for one month – mainly in things like sabotage.'

Shaaban described the political atmosphere in Egypt at the time. Nasser's struggle was going on and a lot was changing. Just a few years earlier (in 1956) Nasser had nationalized the Suez Canal Company and anti-imperialism was sweeping the country. The Egyptian government was redistributing land, and planning industrialization.

After they had spent a short while getting some military training, Shaaban remembered how Ali Sultan had told them 'instead of going to Europe there are other more urgent studies in Zanzibar!' They returned to the Isles.

> There were a lot of dirty tricks going on after the 1961 election. For example, although it had been agreed that after the election we would go back to Cairo to finish our training, Ali Muhsin objected. He sent his own right-wing people whom he controlled. Then Ali Sultan contacted the Cubans and they agreed to give us training in Cuba. We went to Cuba but while we were there, Babu was arrested for sedition, sentenced to 18 months and fined a large sum of money. Some of us in the youth cadres were also charged with 'bringing in seditious materials' and so on …. Ali Muhsin tried to stop us organizing a campaign for Babu's release. He said there was no need. But we did organize a strong campaign.
>
> (interview with Shaaban, 2009)

Babu's arrest in early January 1962 was clearly an effort to paralyze the left as an organized force. The ZNP youth arrested with him were eventually released, but he was not.

The British and the ZNP–ZPPP then conspired to discredit and attack the left. Ali Sultan, who was open in his criticisms of Ali Muhsin and Shamte, was expelled from the ZNP, and Shamte tried, without success, to have him expelled from the FPTU as well. It was, as Khamis remembered, a time of all kinds of dirty tricks. In one significant event described by Ali Sultan (Burgess, 2009: 79), a bundle of papers was thrown on to his bed through an open window of his house. They were letters supposedly signed by him and addressed to the son of the Sultan, to Ali Muhsin, to Shamte and to Karume as leader of the opposition. They said that Ali Sultan and his group of comrades were going to kill them.

Ali Sultan immediately rushed to the FPTU office and showed the letters to Badawi and Khamis who were working there. They told him to burn them immediately. Even as the letters were reduced to ashes, the news came that the police had surrounded his house and were about to search it.

What Makes Someone Guilty of Sedition?

Babu's trial which led to the 18-month sentence was clearly a major court case, and led to an avalanche of British secret telegrams and memos.

Officially, the sedition charge had been brought on an extremely flimsy basis. In the words of a British document (Public Record Office, 1962b) on the *Babu Sedition Trial*: 'Abdul Rahman Mohamed Babu is to be prosecuted for sedition following a statement which appeared in *ZaNews* on the 29th December to the effect that the riots were premeditated and planned by the ASP with the connivance of the "colonial" government.' Since the statement could hardly be regarded as a threat to the state, the real reasons for his arrest were clearly different. The UK intelligence agencies had been keeping an eye on him from his early days in Britain. The UK Foreign Office noted, for example, on February 23, 1962:

> The subject has a long record of Communist activity dating back to 1951 ... he is believed to be a member of the British Communist Party and ... to have lectured at their school in Hastings on the 'Problems of Imperialism'... quickly established contact with the WFTU and other Communist organizations .... He became the principal East Africa correspondent for the New China News Agency, the editor of *ZaNews*, a particularly scurrilous pro-Communist news sheet and most significantly General Secretary of the ZNP .... Was largely instrumental in setting up the ZNP Cairo office as a staging point for students travelling along the iron curtain countries pipeline .... Subject attended an anti-atom bomb conference in Japan in July 1961, and strongly supported a resolution

that none of the countries present should allow American consulates or bases in their countries. Shortly after his return an abortive attempt was made to set fire to the American Consulate in Zanzibar.

(Public Record Office, 1962b)

(This 'abortive attempt' was an unsuccessful sabotage attempt by some ZNP youth who were also involved in a small, independent and more or less ad hoc anti-imperialist organization called the Zanzibar Action Group.)

The same document also noted: 'Subject has considerable following among the younger element of the ZNP and the ZNP-supporting Federation of Progressive Trade Unions and is known to have secret contacts with the ASP-supporting Zanzibar and Pemba Federation of Labour.'

Babu had arranged for the radical lawyer Ralph Milner to defend him, but the British prevented Milner from entering Zanzibar, the Secretary of State for the Colonies noting in a telegram to the Acting British Resident, 'Reliable information here indicates, Milner still active member of Communist Party' (Public Record Office, 1962b).

Kanti Kotecha, who was the government's prosecutor at the Appeal Court, told me in an interview in November 2010 that Babu's case was first tried before the Zanzibar High Court where there was no jury. He continued:

> This is where Babu was found guilty and sentenced to nine months in jail. The case was then appealed to the East African Court of Appeal. Babu had hired a prominent barrister, O'Donovan from London [who presumably was a replacement for Milner], to represent him in the appeal. I represented the government. ... I have absolutely no doubt in my mind he was guilty under the law. Of course, the sedition laws of those days were very much in favour of the government. This is probably still the case even under the independent government .... All three judges in the Court of Appeal were British. They were all unanimous in their opinion. There was no dissenting opinion.

Revealing his own approach, Kotecha added:

> The mistake many researchers make is to concentrate on Babu and fail to realize the overall significance of communist infiltration and training of Zanzibaris in communist ideology by Cuba, East Germany, the Soviet Union and China. Upon their return, these comrades made peaceful and non-revolutionary operation of political processes and

good governance almost impossible. Instead of trying to prosecute them individually, the government might have been better off to have declared a state of emergency and put away for a period of years all those who were unwilling to continue on a peaceful and democratic path to independence. At that point, however, the British (especially the colonial secretary [Ian] Macleod) just wanted to just wash their hands off, give the Zanzibaris independence, and leave.

The Lancaster House Constitutional Conference

At the end of March 1962 a Constitutional Conference was convened at Lancaster House. Babu was allowed to attend on bond and only as an observer. During the conference he received information that the British had told the right-wing leadership of the ZNP–ZPPP that the party would not be permitted to inherit power if they did not get rid of the leftists, and that Muhsin and Shamte had agreed to collaborate with the colonialists on this.

Eager to hand over official power and presumably more confident about a government which would not include the leftists, the British suggested a coalition government. However the ZNP–ZPPP were not willing to offer the ASP more than three ministerial positions out of nine, while the ASP wanted equal representation and continued to demand an election before independence.

There were, of course, in addition, a number of essential differences in public policy between the two sides over issues such as land distribution and the racial composition of the civil service. Othman Shariff's speech on behalf of the ASP on the first day of the conference, highlighted these differences:

> Economically, socially and politically the distribution is rather in the inverse proportion to the population ... 80% of the fertile land and the bulk of the trade and industry are in the hands of the minority and ... practically all the administrative positions of importance are occupied by them. This state of affairs calls for adjustment and change.
> (quoted in Lofchie, 1965: 215)

He argued forcefully for a thoroughgoing land reform programme among other changes. This stand on land reform was one which had long divided the ASP, with the right wing led by Karume opposing land reform – perhaps reflecting his own class position more than anything else. As for the ZNP, the progressives within it were in favour

THE THREAT OF LIBERATION

Babu arriving at a celebration on April 29, 1963 to mark his release from jail. Qullatein Badawi is on the right facing the camera.
Source: Mohamed Amin/Camerapix.

of land reform but were unable to take any stand on this. As a result the ZNP–ZPPP came out publicly as completely opposed to land reform.

Khamis remembered that period:

> There was a clear line between our thinking and the thinking of the leaders of ZNP on the question of land reform, but it was not possible at that point to take a stand. Land redistribution is part of socialism, and so of course, we wanted it. But we knew that if we put it forward then, we would not succeed, because at that time the party was dominated by landlords. At the beginning [in the early days of the ZNP] landlords were few in the party but by this time Ali Mushin was bringing in a large number of landlords and other people purely from a racial point of view, Arabs related to him and so on.
> (interview with Khamis Ameir, 2009)

Deadlock followed the Lancaster House Conference. Finally, in March 1963, Duncan Sandys, the British secretary of state for the Colonies,

A huge crowd eagerly waiting to welcome Babu in front of the ZNP headquarters at Darajani opposite the Bharmal Building
© Bettmann/CORBIS.

visited Zanzibar and imposed a compromise plan under which self-government would be introduced in late June and followed two weeks later by a general election.

A Revolutionary Party Is Launched

Babu's release to a tumultuous welcome on April 29, 1963 recharged the spirits of YOU members and other progressive people in Zanzibar. The left began to take on the ZNP right wing more vigorously over a number of key issues. In the run-up to the July 1963 election, they argued that the party must return to its previous anti-imperialist position, that despite the electoral alliance with the ZPPP, it must disassociate itself from the ZPPP's pro-imperialist and anti-mainlander political stand, and publish its manifesto stating its position quite clearly on the land question, the role of the working class and the economic priorities of the new government. And last but not least, in a gesture to its previous multiracial stand, the party must field progressive candidates to stand in safe constituencies instead of using ethnicity to weigh in favour of candidates (by fielding Arab candidates in predominantly Arab constituencies and African candidates in predominantly African constituencies). They argued passionately that ethnicity should not determine who would stand where, and only by standing progressive candidates who might well be of a different ethnicity from the majority in their constituencies could the ZNP call itself multiracial.

The right wing of the ZNP rejected these arguments. Their view was that the ZNP–ZPPP alliance was something to be celebrated, and the coalition government of the two parties would draw in all 'genuine Zanzibaris', leading to a collapse of the ASP.

Finally, in June, at a pre-election party conference where the leaders were to seek a mandate for the forthcoming Constitutional Conference in Lancaster House, the left resigned en masse. The very next day, a new revolutionary party, the Umma Party, was launched.

The effect was dramatic. Youth particularly from the working class and peasantry of all political parties and racial groupings were galvanized into action. The first mass rally on the second day after the party's formation attracted several thousand. Its political vitality was such that in less than a week it had attracted hundreds of new members from all classes and racial groups. It had a huge impact on the political scene. On the one hand it brought home to people the reality of the situation on the eve of independence – that the forces who were earlier in league with the colonialists were now in the major political parties trying to hijack independence and push the country back to neocolonialism. On the other hand it also brought hope and a fresh approach by making people aware that the future could be different – that, with their involvement, Zanzibar could be prevented from going down the neocolonial path and instead could develop as an independent socialist nation.

In the next few months, the Umma Party began to widen its base. Its programme committed it to being a 'conscious vanguard of the oppressed people of Zanzibar [representing] the broad interests of the African people who today are bearing the brunt of economic oppression resulting from foreign colonialism and local feudalism' and to 'fighting imperialist oppression with the ultimate aim of socialism' in Zanzibar (see Appendix 1). Its aims included securing 'the unity of all the people of Zanzibar and unity of people of East Africa and the whole of Africa on the basis of Pan-Africanism.'

The party reached out to FPTU members, the vast majority

of whom left the ZNP and joined Umma, leaving the ZNP–ZPPP government effectively without trade union support. It also developed close links with the ZPFL, the ASP-affiliated trade union federation. As Lofchie pointed out:

> the rank and file and the leadership of the ZPFL were predominantly mainland Africans, and their political sympathies were wholly with the ASP. The FPTU ... [had previously reflected the anti-mainland African prejudices of the ZNP, but] now with this obstacle removed common ideological sentiments began to draw the movements together.
> (Lofchie, 1965: 261)

Khamis, the general secretary of the FPTU, confirmed this: 'The Umma Party was a small party but it was backed strongly by the trade unions, not only the FPTU but also workers from the other trade union federation the ZPFL, although they supported the ASP' (interview with Khamis Ameir, 2009).

While continuing to refer to the ZNP–ZPPP coalition as 'moderates', Lofchie was impressed, almost against his will, by the Umma Party which, he noted, included among its activists several of Zanzibar's most effective organizers and was 'highly disciplined and tightly integrated; it possessed a powerful, unifying Marxist ideology and enjoyed considerable *esprit de corps*' (Lofchie, 1965: 262). Although he seems to have forgotten to mention Babu in the first 258 pages of his 281-page book, Lofchie did eventually note that:

> Babu ... was universally acknowledged as the organizational genius of Zanzibar politics, and in a brief time had placed Umma at the head of practically all militant opposition groups... [with] strong working ties with the largest trade unions, the press and even with several influential members of the ASP.
> (Lofchie, 1965: 258)

On December 10, 1964, the British finally granted formal independence to Zanzibar. With the Sultan as head of state given the power to negotiate his successor, it was the kind of structure they needed in order to keep control of the islands.

Repression now escalated to unprecedented levels. Travel to the mainland or Europe was restricted, search and seizure became common, and Ali Muhsin, the minister for internal affairs, awarded himself almost arbitrary repressive power. Two bills were announced which would give the government power to ban any political party and proscribe any newspaper it considered dangerous.

The Umma Party, aware that it was to be the target of these laws, formed a tactical alliance with the ASP, the official opposition, and at the same time set up a journalists' organization, the Zanzibar Journalists Organisation, which brought together the opposition press – not only *Za News* and *Sauti ya Umma* (the Voice of Umma) but *Africa Kwetu*, the ASP supporting newspaper, *Jamhuri* (The Republic) which was run by a former ZPPP leader who had joined the ASP, and a number of other magazines and newspapers. Through these Umma sought to mobilize people outside parliament and campaign against the proposed new laws.

However, despite considerable opposition, the government succeeded in pushing through the acts. At the same time it decided to completely restructure the police force simply because a majority of them were from the mainland and hence regarded as 'untrustworthy' by the ZNP–ZPPP rulers. Senior police officers and rank and file police, many of whom had been recruited by the British in Tanganyika, Kenya and Nyasaland, all lost their jobs without compensation. Not surprisingly they responded with anger and resentment. Many of them were discharged without being repatriated, and this group, who were trained in the use of weapons, remained in Zanzibar.

The justice and democracy which people had fought for in the anti-colonial struggle had faded from the horizon. On January 6, 1964, the Umma Party was banned as had been anticipated, its daily news bulletin proscribed and assets confiscated. Almost immediately afterwards, the police raided the homes of its leaders. In Babu's house, having failed to find anything incriminating, they unearthed an ancient and unusable pistol, probably a relic of the previous resident – a colonial officer. This discovery of 'a gun' was noted by the police.

The next day sympathisers of the Umma Party in the police warned Babu that he was about to be charged with treason – a charge which carried a mandatory death penalty – and urged him to leave Zanzibar. To avoid arrest and try to find a lawyer who would defend him if he was charged, Babu decided to escape to Dar es Salaam. It was a historic trip by canoe which has become the stuff of legend in Zanzibar – retold with varying degrees of accuracy. In fact, it was made possible because Badawi managed to get hold of an outrigger canoe with the help of Saleh Saadalla and Abdulaziz Twala (progressive members of the ASP).

He and Babu then travelled to Fumba, a fishing village in south-west Zanzibar, where the canoe was waiting, and it was from here that Babu, accompanied by Ali Mahfoudh, made the journey across the channel to Dar es Salaam.

Tension was high, and rumours started circulating that some members of the ASP youth league and lumpen elements were planning to burn the city down in the next few days. The Zanzibar revolution was round the corner.

CHAPTER THREE

The Zanzibar Revolution and Imperialist Fears

Although Umma members frequently discussed revolutionary tactics, they neither planned the insurrection in Zanzibar nor knew anything concrete about it. Babu was still away in Dar es Salaam when it erupted on January 12, 1964.

On the night of Saturday January 11, Karume and Aboud Jumbe, who was at that time the ASP's chief whip in the legislature, informed the Special Branch that they had information that there was going to be some trouble that night, and that neither they nor the ASP were involved (Shivji, 2008: 47). Clearly Karume, at least, was worried that if the revolution failed he might be blamed, and was taking the precaution of distancing himself. As a result of this information J. M. Sullivan, the commissioner of police, sent a few guards to Ali Muhsin's house and the Sultan's palace.

The 'trouble' Karume had warned the commissioner about came at 2.00am on Sunday morning, with the Ziwani barracks and its armoury being attacked and taken over. There followed an attack on the Mtoni barracks.

The British government's immediate reaction to the insurrection early on 12 January was to reinforce the Zanzibar government's call to Nyerere and Kenyatta for police reinforcements and urge the US State Department to do the same. Its primary concern at this stage was for British lives and property, and not about supporting the Zanzibar government (about which it seems to have been somewhat lukewarm). A few hours later, the High Commissioner sent a panicky cable to the British War Office asking for British troops to be sent:

> [The] Prime Minister has appealed to me for immediate dispatch of British troops on grounds that British lives and property are or soon will be in danger. I appreciate the constitutional difficulty in providing British forces to an independent state. But situation is likely to become serious unless reinforcements reach Zanzibar promptly from Kenya and Tanganyika to whom the Zanzibar authorities have also appealed. If you do not feel able to respond to this appeal at once please arrange at least for the stationing of air transport at Dar es Salaam.
> (quoted in Wilson, 1989: 13)

The same night the US State Department received the news that Kenyan troops were flying to Zanzibar, that the NASA station had not been touched and also that a combined Kenyan, Tanganyikan and Ugandan force would be sent to 'restore order in Zanzibar'. However, despite this the US Joint Chiefs of Staff ordered the destroyer *USS Manley*, which was stationed at Mombasa, to go to Zanzibar. Four hours later *USS Manley* was ordered to turn back, and four hours later again ordered to sail once more to Zanzibar. In fact, no European was harmed, and nor was any property belonging to Europeans damaged in course of the uprising (Shivji, 2008: 49).

The 'rebels', as the British chose to call them, were mainly ASP Youth League members together with a large number of angry lumpen unemployed youth supported by disaffected ex-police officers. They secured an initial advantage over the newly recruited police force, but after a while, using ambush tactics, the police began to shoot at and kill the inexperienced young men. This was when the Umma Party Youth entered the arena. They took charge, showing the untrained youth the strategy and tactics of urban warfare. Hashil Seif Hashil, a Central Committee member of the Umma Youth who had earlier, as a ZNP member, received military training and other education in Cuba, recalled in an interview in 1988:

> That first night there was chaos everywhere. Many people just did not know what they were doing. One of the things the Umma Party did was explain the purpose of the revolution – it was not to kill, rape, or steal, but to change the country. Some people listened but obviously not everyone.
> The Umma Youth were assigned missions by the ASP who did not

know how to perform these missions themselves .... Three of us trained in Cuba were sent to the prison. It was a difficult operation, those who tried before had been killed – but we did it. Then they asked us to take over Malinde police station; here too people had been killed. It was in an open area near the Stone Town, near the port area, so we decided to approach it at night. This was on the night of January 12. It was led by another Umma cadre, Amour Dugheshi.

(quoted in Wilson, 1989: 12)

Hashil went to Cable and Wireless, the radio station for all external communications. It was in Stone Town, in a ZNP area. As he recollected:

I had 12 people with me. We split ourselves into two groups and approached it in camouflage .... Anyway, we succeeded. The person in charge was an Englishman. We did not want to intimidate him; he was in his underpants. We let him take his trousers and nothing else.

(quoted in Wilson, 1989: 12)

Looking back at that time, it is evident that the Umma Party had three important roles. First, it secured the revolution – the uprising would have simply been crushed without the party. Second, as Babu wrote, it helped to transform a 'lumpen, in many ways apolitical uprising into a popular, anti-imperialist revolution ... the intervention of the socialist forces [created] ... more favourable conditions for revolutionary and indeed socialist prospects throughout the region' (Babu, 1991: 245). And third, because the party included Arabs and Asians, it decreased the extent of ethnic polarization and prevented the attacks on Arabs from becoming the central thrust of the uprising.

As Mahmood Mamdani put it:

the Umma Party and its active participation in the ... revolution was the first step in setting the Zanzibari Revolution of 1964 on a course different from the Rwandese 'Social Revolution' of 1959: whereas the divide between revolution and counter revolution crystallized as a Hutu–Tutsi divide in 1959 Rwanda, matters stood a little differently in Zanzibar of 1964. It is because of Babu and the Umma Party that the Arab in Zanzibar unlike the Tutsi in Rwanda, stood as an organized force, not just on the side of privilege, but also that of the revolution.

(Mamdani, 1996)

However, despite their efforts, the Umma cadres were only partially successful in stemming the violence against Arabs unleashed as a result of the ASP's years of racist propaganda. Without entering the debate about numbers, it is clear that killings were widespread and so were rapes and abductions of Arab and Asian women. These were, and were seen as, attacks on the entire Arab population, the majority of whom were neither oppressors nor wealthy.

A curtain of silence was drawn over the assaults on women, perhaps because in Zanzibar, as in other deeply patriarchal, feudal societies, rape is taken to be a sign of collective dishonour. When a woman is raped the entire family sees itself as shamed and humiliated. Brothers, fathers and husbands see themselves as having failed (Napoli and Saleh, 2005). At the same time, patriarchy stipulates that men of a particular group have ownership of 'their' women, and women's bodies therefore are available to these men and denied to others. It is this that was central to the violence faced by women in Zanzibar.

'A Week of Grievous Shame for the Nation'

In the early morning of January 12, with the smoke and chaos of the revolution still in the air, Babu returned from Dar es Salaam to Zanzibar. He was accompanied by Karume, who had fled the insurrection late on Sunday night. In the next two days the membership of the Revolutionary Council and the Cabinet were agreed. In both, the ASP was by far the dominant party. In fact the Revolutionary Council had only two Umma Party members, Babu and Khamis Ameir. The new cabinet consisted of Karume as president; Abdullah Hanga, vice president; Babu, minister of foreign affairs and trade; Othman Shariff, minister of education and culture; Aboud Jumbe, minister of health and welfare; Idrisa Wakil, minister of communication and works; Saleh Saadalla, minister of agriculture; and Abdulazizi Ali Twala and Hasan Nassor Moyo as junior ministers.

Pemba had not been involved in the insurrection, and it was only after a week that the revolution was consolidated there. Although Ali Sultan Issa became the administrator of Pemba, clearly here too the balance of power was in the hands of the ASP.

Despite the minority of posts held by Umma Party members, the events in Zanzibar were seen by the British and Americans as a deeply worrying 'communist takeover'. The British were also unhappy because as J. K. Hickman, a diplomat who served in the Commonwealth Relations Office, East Africa Department, remembered:

Babu with Karume
Source: Mohamed Amin/Camerapix.

> The Secretary of State, Duncan Sandys, was extremely reluctant to give any recognition to this revolutionary government. He regarded himself as committed completely to the Sultan because he had so recently signed an agreement with the Sultan and he wasn't prepared to do anything to contradict or take away from that agreement, so we were in an ambiguous situation for a long time.
>
> (Hickman, 1995)

The next few days saw a hurricane of secret messages and plans pass between the UK and US governments and US embassies in East Africa, which made it plain that Nyerere had emerged as a key ally of the West. On January 15, for example, Dean Rusk, the US secretary of state, cabled US embassies in East Africa pointing out that while Uganda and Kenya had recognized the revolutionary government, Tanganyika had not done so. And perhaps the governments of Kenya and Uganda could be encouraged by President Nyerere to join him in supporting this policy line with the new regime.

However, dramatic events were round the corner which would both reveal Nyerere's weak position internally and consolidate his dependence on the United Kingdom and the United States.

These events began on January 19, when soldiers in the Colito barracks in Dar es Salaam, angry about their low pay and the retention of European officers in top posts, mutinied. This was accompanied by a police rebellion and dockworkers' strike, and the possibility of other unions uniting to call a general strike. All these protests expressed the anger felt by many in Tanganyika about the continuation of colonial structures in an independent country.

Through these protests, Nyerere remained confined in State House. Eventually, on the evening of January 24, he sent a written request to the British government for military assistance against Tanganyika's own people. The next day a British force did indeed land and bombard the barracks, crushing the mutiny. On January 26, Nyerere finally addressed the nation. His speech, despite its moralistic, schoolteacherish tone and its petulant justification of his actions, was as close as could be to an admission of his powerlessness and dependence on the West in the face of a situation which was truly out of his control:

> I am told that there is already foolish talk that the British have come back to rule Tanganyika again. This is rubbish …. Any independent country is able to ask for the help of another independent country. Asking for help in this way is not something to be proud of. I do not want any person to think I was happy in making this request. The whole week has been a week of grievous shame for our nation.
> (quoted in Wilson, 1989: 30)

The United States Formulates New Strategies for Africa

Meanwhile the United States, panic-stricken by the possibility that the Zanzibar situation was linked to the Tanganyikan mutiny which might well spread throughout East Africa, formulated a new policy paper about the disturbing signs in three East African countries which could require the country to act urgently and make contingency plans.

The paper identified various action points, among which were protecting the *Mercury* tracking station and boosting Nyerere, because 'Our central purpose is to strengthen the position of Nyerere .... Nyerere may well need elements of a new program to assert his power' (quoted in Wilson, 1989: 26).

In response to these threats, the US State Department put in place a two-pronged strategy. First, it pushed the British to send in the military to invade the islands (the so-called Zanzibar Action Plan), an action it hoped Karume would support. Second, it tried to manipulate Karume and others to agree to a union under the 'moderate' Nyerere. In addition, Dean Rusk cabled US ambassadors in Tanganyika, Uganda and Kenya on March 5, directing them to urge Nyerere, Obote and Kenyatta to explain to Karume the dangers involved in the ASP's dependence on Babu, and suggesting a Zanzibar–Tanganyika federation:

> the big problem is that Karume himself has great confidence in and dependence on Babu ... also that Nyerere has said that Karume needs Babu, who despite his background, can and must be worked with .... *Would it be useful to raise with Nyerere, despite his previous objection, the idea of a Zanzibar Tanganyika Federation as a possible way of strengthening Karume and reducing Babu's influence? Such action can also help Nyerere's own position.*
> (quoted in Wilson, 1989: 48, italics added)

A couple of weeks earlier, the key US manipulator and destabilizer of progressive governments, Frank Carlucci, had arrived in Zanzibar. He had come directly from the Congo where the CIA had been deeply involved in the overthrow of Lumumba, and this perhaps shows just how seriously the Zanzibar revolution was being viewed by the State Department. The Congo had been only the latest in Carlucci's record of destabilizations, preceded by Brazil and Portugal. His aim now, in his own words, was to prevent Zanzibar becoming 'an African Cuba from which sedition would have spread to the continent' (quoted in Wilson, 1987: 41). He and other US officials began to bolster Karume's position, creating splits between him and other leaders of the Revolutionary Government and trying to develop an even closer relationship with Nyerere.

Early Days of the People's Republic of Zanzibar

Despite the plotting going on behind their backs, which they suspected but had no concrete information on, and the fact that there were only

Che Guevara and Babu, relaxing after the first UNCTAD conference in Geneva, July 1964
(Photographer unknown.)

a few of their members in government, the Umma Party succeeded in bringing a number of progressive changes to Zanzibar in the early days of the People's Republic. The most important, a new economic strategy, was central to the future that they planned for Zanzibar. For this, Babu planned and began to establish a framework, using Zanzibar's exports to enable changes to the economic structure and to develop the home market. We shall look at these plans in the last section of this chapter.

At the same time a new foreign policy was formulated, specifying fraternal relations with socialist countries and a more cautious approach towards the imperialist camp. The Zanzibar delegation took a leading role in supporting Cuba at the first United Nations Conference on Trade and Development (UNCTAD) in Geneva in February 1964, and was instrumental in the formation of the 'Group of 77'.[1] It was at this conference that close relations with Che Guevara and other Cuban leaders were first established. They were the beginning of a long-standing relationship between Zanzibar and Cuba.

There were also important changes on the domestic front, which included reorganizing the police force in collaboration with the Tanganyikan government, setting up a People's Liberation Army and abolishing all privileges at the expense of the state, with 'no special status for anyone, however high in authority even Karume, the President, was driving his own car, with no outriders, no flags, or any of the pompous paraphernalia so common in neo-colonial countries' (Babu, 1991).

However, this atmosphere was not to last long. Existing tensions within the ASP between men like Othman Shariff and Karume started to escalate, and Karume began to consolidate his own position with the help of a small right-wing inner circle, the so-called Committee of Fourteen. This also inevitably affected the ASP's relationship with the Umma Party, although Umma cadres, particularly Babu, did try to intervene to prevent the escalation of conflict within the ASP.

Increasingly, Umma cadres found themselves being prevented from implementing their policies. Khamis told me, for example, that:

> Our trade union, the FRTU, requested the government to increase the minimum wages from 15 shillings to 20 shillings a day, which was fair at that time. President Karume called me as the general secretary and Mohamed Mfaume as the president of the FRTU and gave us a serious warning, telling us furiously to declare to the Revolutionary Council that we had no confidence in the government. (We knew that if we did this he would use it against us.) We were advised by other colleagues to go to see him at State House in the evening and explain to him again that the increase in the minimum wage would boost the Revolutionary Council and win the support of the workers. We found Karume in a good mood. He told us that he was running a workers' government and many good things would come. But no wages were increased and it was the beginning of the destruction of the trade unions of Zanzibar.
>
> (interview with Khamis Ameir, 2009)

(Karume was to ban trade union activity, and also youth and women's organizations, completely by May 1965.) Khamis wanted to resign from the Revolutionary Council but Saleh Sadalla persuaded him not to.

By March 1964, Karume had become increasingly close to the United States, although Zanzibar was also receiving aid from China, the Soviet Union and East Germany (a country which Karume personally greatly admired). His relationship with the Americans is illustrated by another incident related by Khamis:

> When we issued a statement on behalf of the Federation of Revolutionary Trade Unions against US imperialism in Vietnam, American deputy consul Petterson went to Karume and threatened him. He told him that the US Government want to help the Revolutionary Government of Zanzibar but our trade unions are attacking the US and it would be difficult to obtain help if such 'abuses' continue.
> (interview with Khamis Ameir, 2009)

Karume panicked and again called Khamis and Mfaume and 'warned' them aggressively. Clearly his approach had changed considerably since mid-January when he had been personally involved in expelling US consul Fredrick Picard for interfering in the internal affairs of Zanzibar.

'Racial Strategy Acted Out on Women's Bodies'

The sexual abuse of young Arab, Shirazi and Asian women by ASP politicians also became fairly common in the months after the revolution, and was effectively institutionalized in the form of forced marriages through the deliberate misuse of a new law.

The fact that despite the numerous historical studies of the revolution and its aftermath, few academics have touched in any detail on this subject tells us something, perhaps, about the way women's experiences have been systematically sidelined. Salma Maoulidi's work is an exception. She discusses the distortion and abuse of the Equality, Reconciliation of Zanzibar Peoples Decree No. 6, 1964 which was passed after the revolution, noting that while:

> the Decree claimed to try to break down racial and class barriers 'by allowing those in love who faced unreasonable opposition from their families the possibility to get married by the state without the approval of the legal guardian [... in fact, it launched a] major racial strategy acted out on the bodies of women ...[and became] an avenue through

which older men, most of whom were already married, preyed on young 'virgins' to satisfy their sexual appetites or settle old scores. Members of the Revolutionary Council led by example, many forcibly marrying women previously denied to them, especially Arab and Indian girls and some women from prominent Shirazi families.

(Maoulidi, 2011)

Throughout this period Nyerere took no public stand on the subject. In Zanzibar, these policies were still being publicly glorified, as recently as April 2010, by Hasan Nassor Moyo, who had been the first president of the ASP Youth League and later minister of state (Naluyaga, 2010).

The violence that followed the revolution left deep scars. Race remained a strong underlying current in the everyday life and politics of Zanzibar. In the administration, in the months after the revolution, as Khamis told me:

> There were racial policies at every level .... Many Arabs left for Oman or Kenya – those who remained were not economically well off, so you could not point a finger at them and say they were exploiting Africans .... Even today you feel it, though it is much less .... Even now in the army there is not a single Arab or Asian. In the administration there are very few Asians. They tried to Africanize it and that caused problems. There was corruption and the government departments were filled with the sons and daughters of top people, they were unskilled and also they were undisciplined, they wouldn't go to work on time. And the administration basically collapsed. A few rich Asians remained, they were the biggest supporters of the ASP.
>
> (interview with Khamis Ameir, 2009)

The Demise of the Legal System

If there was an inherent ambiguity in the new law affecting marriage which could be abused, the same was true, in different ways, of some of the other laws passed by the new government reflecting the contradictions between the majority of ASP members and the minority of Umma Party members.

Many of them were drafted by a lawyer who had been an adviser to the ASP at the Lancaster House Conference and was close to the colonial government, Thomas Franck. Franck had worked, often in conjunction with Lancaster House, to produce legal frameworks for countries such as Zimbabwe and Sierra Leone, and was a legal adviser to Kenya, Mauritius and Chad. These countries emerged from colonialism holding on to the repressive laws they had inherited from colonial regimes. He was so close to the United States that George Ball noted appreciatively in a secret cable that Franck had 'successfully resisted drafting decree incorporating People's Republic into State's name' (quoted in Wilson, 1989: 46).

The new laws, in Zanzibar, appeared to set up a democratic state based on the rule of law, with an independent judiciary, and proclaimed that the Constituent Assembly of the Zanzibar People would be convened by January 1965 to promulgate the Constitution of Zanzibar. But the laws passed between January 1964 and March 1964 were far from democratic. For example, the High Court Decree, as Shivji wrote:

> established the High Court as a 'superior court of record and, save as otherwise provided by the President, shall have all the powers of such a court' ... [this] in effect ... established a judicial system in the tradition of the common law. There was of course one exception. The President could decide otherwise, and later ... the judicial system was whittled away by the decisions of the President.
>
> (Shivji, 2008: 59)

Almost all decrees passed between January 31 and March 25 confirmed the president's total power. The Preventative Detention Decree gave him the power to incarcerate anyone for as long as he chose to, if he thought the person was acting, or was even likely to act, in a manner dangerous to peace and good order or to the security of the state. Other decrees gave the president the power to command the armed forces and appoint ministers as he thought fit, and to confiscate and acquire property 'in the national interest' and without compensation if he thought it would not cause 'undue hardship' to the owner (Shivji, 2008: 60).

The Dissolution of the Umma Party

For the Umma Party, the passage of these laws, the constant obstruction of progressive measures, the veiled and increasingly open conflict between the ASP leadership and Umma members in government, and the growing power of men around Karume (the brutal and sadistic so-called Committee of Fourteen who were members of the ASP Youth League) were ominous signs. They were aware that all other political parties were banned and that if open conflict flared up, the Umma Party was likely to be banned as well. They knew also that if they were banned again they had no means of going underground.

In a letter to Karim Essack, written in 1982, Babu explained these problems further within a more general framework:

> to go underground in the circumstances of our countries you need: (a) fairly large and complex urban centres with some support from the people, (b) wide-scale rural support among the peasants who already have some confidence in proletarian leadership and (c) a pre-existent party organization with minimum rural and urban infrastructure ... to go underground without these conditions ... is to condemn the movement to the negative role of 'roving bands'.
>
> (Babu, [1982a] 2002: 278)

Under these conditions, caught between two harsh alternatives, Babu, never one for 'pursuing dream worlds', had to make a realistic decision. The Umma Party was dissolved on March 8, 1964. This was seen to be the only way that the left forces could continue to function and pursue their objectives in Zanzibar. Although the party was officially dissolved, Umma Party members continued to function as a political group, if not a party. While the dissolution of the party clearly gave Karume more administrative control over them, it also gave the ex-Umma Party members a greater chance of activism within the trade union movement and other mass organizations, which were not to be banned for more than a year. Chase (1976: 17) suggests that the dissolution of the Umma Party also had some distinct advantages for the left because it opened the door to greater organizational unity 'between the ex-Umma Party cadres and the militant left-wing of the ASP'. Its long-term implications were not favourable to the Karume bloc of the ASP, and 'this was a fact clearly discerned by the astute Karume who, shortly after this, actively 'encouraged' major Umma leaders to depart Zanzibar' (Chase, 1976: 17).

The Zanzibar that Might Have Been

Even in this tense atmosphere the ex-Umma cadres continued to try to push forward the agenda they had struggled for. The most striking example of this was on the economic front. Here Babu, as minister of foreign affairs and trade, took some remarkable first steps towards implementing his vision for an economically independent Zanzibar.

His starting points were first, that Zanzibar had an opportunity to break completely with colonialism, and second, that the Isles had at that time considerable resources – a population with skills and sophistication, and internal capital. With these unique assets, the two economic sectors that 'create new wealth' – agriculture and industry – could be activated. Everything else – banking, insurance, commerce, trade, tourism, social services, the home market – depended on these two vital sectors.

For assistance in planning the new economy Babu turned to China – a country which had not only confronted underdevelopment and imperialist plunder but was, at that time, the only third world country that had developed an economy independent of external resources. Babu described this in an interview in 1988:

> The Chinese produced a very interesting report designed to restructure the economy of Zanzibar. They told us don't nationalize indiscriminately, concentrate only on major items. The state must control the export of cloves and copra because they are the major exports and control sugar and rice because they are the main items of import. Leave the rest to private dealers and small businesses. They warned us against unprincipled nationalization. (Later, we found it to be true, because in Tanzania experiments in nationalization led to economic disaster.) ... The Chinese suggested an economy which was internally integrated and gradually restructured to become less and less dependent on cloves and agricultural products and producing more food.... They also suggested we develop local industry. Zanzibar already had some viable industries – we produced soap, for example – now we began to think of producing textiles with cotton from the mainland.
>
> (quoted in Wilson, 1989: 59)

The plan was soon to be put into action. In the early weeks of April, Babu went to Indonesia, then a major importer of Zanzibar's cloves. A trilateral trade-cum-industrial arrangement was agreed with the Indonesian government, under which Zanzibar would supply Indonesia with cloves of a certain agreed value, Indonesia would supply Germany [the German Democratic Republic] with raw materials of equal value, and Germany in turn would supply Zanzibar with machines to develop a variety of industries – textiles, building and construction, edible oil milling, machine tools and machines to modernize and develop clove distillation and clove products. These exchanges were to take place at equivalent values and prices based on the prevailing world market prices of the goods exchanged. In this way, existing skills would have been utilized and thousands of jobs created while promoting modern technologies and helping Zanzibar modernize its agricultural base. It was never to be, as Babu was to write later:

> Just as we were celebrating the good news we were taking home about the dynamic future we were going to usher in – hey presto! Like a bolt from the blue came the news of imminent formation of the Union between Zanzibar and Tanganyika. When we arrived home the situation was like a coup d'etat: the atmosphere was tense and generally everything had changed; there was a pervading sight of winners and losers in everybody's faces; in short everything had diametrically changed – virtually from revolution to counter-revolution. It was irrelevant to talk about the good tidings from Indonesia because there was obviously no possibility for the plan to be implemented as arranged. First because the formation of the Union deprived us of our sovereign authority to enter into such a binding arrangement; secondly the priorities of the new situation were drastically different; and thirdly because the personnel, both at political and administrative levels, were disrupted and could not maintain the continuity essential for such an undertaking. All hopes were dashed; a great historical opportunity had been missed.
>
> (Babu, 1994: 31)

CHAPTER FOUR

The Union with Tanganyika

The events of the fortnight prior to the Union are particularly interesting, because as we shall see, declassified CIA and US State Department documents provide us with a glimpse of the methods used by the United States, many of which are still being used today. These cables illustrate too how Tanganyika and Zanzibar were located in the imperialist vision of East Africa.

The Americans and the British were considering a number of different strategies and plans. There was the possibility, for example, of uniting the 'moderate' governments of Kenya, Uganda and Tanganyika in an East African Federation and drawing in Zanzibar to neutralize it. This was still in the air as late as mid-April 1964, but appearing less likely.

There was also the possibility of British military intervention, discussed in a paper from the Bureau of Intelligence and Research:

> Zanzibar in six months could be Africa's first Communist-aligned state – in fact though not in name. That contingency could be nipped by a British expeditionary force and Babu's replacement by genuine moderates acceptable to Zanzibar's Afro Shirazi Party. However, President Karume ... is unlikely to issue the appeal for intervention ...; nor apart from Karume is there readily or clearly available a 'moderate' successor to Babu and his leftist clique who retain the essential loyalty of Zanzibar's black inhabitants, yet avoid the stigma of counter-revolution.
> (quoted in Wilson, 1989: 65)

And then there was the possibility, as William Leonhart, the US ambassador to Tanganyika, was able to report to the State Department a few days later, that 'consistent with rumours in London ... Babu will not be permitted return to Zanzibar' (quoted in Wilson, 1989: 73).

'Eliminating' Babu was also being considered, with William Attwood, the US ambassador to Kenya, discussing it with Colin Legum, a journalist with the *Observer*, whom the Americans consulted from time to time. Attwood reported to Washington that Legum had told him 'elimination Babu only solution' (quoted in Wilson, 1989: 71).

However, on April 19 Leonhart reported that things had moved on very quickly, in an apparently unfathomable way. Orders had been given for charter flights to remove Tanganyikan-government-assisted police from Zanzibar to Dar es Salaam. This was followed by Karume travelling to Dar es Salaam, apparently on a secret mission, since the press had not been alerted. Soon after, the order for the charter flights was cancelled. It was Colin Legum, strangely enough, who was able to explain the real reason for these goings-on in an article for the *Observer* in London: '[Nyerere's] first intervention came ... when, in an attempt to stir Karume into an awareness of what was happening, he threatened to withdraw 300 Tanganyikan police .... Karume responded to the warning. He willingly agreed to negotiate with Nyerere' (quoted in Wilson, 1989: 74).

Nyerere's Progressive Cult

Given that Nyerere was obviously under tremendous pressure from the Americans and British to help neutralize Zanzibar, and that he felt obligated to the West for rescuing him during the Colito mutiny, he could hardly be considered to be an independent actor over Zanzibar. This is confirmed over and over again by US documents. For example, the US ambassador in Tanganyika, Leonhart, in a cable to the State Department commented on April 27, 'I believe that it is essential that Nyerere be given the maximum quiet support from the beginning', and on April 29:

> Nyerere's willingness shoulder entire Zanzibar problem stakes Tanganyikan security on faith in will and capacity of West .... My primary recommendation is that we give Nyerere an affirmative response before the weekend on subjects he raised today. For maximum effect this should be ... an assurance that the Free World would commit to URTZ (United Republic of Tanganyika and Zanzibar) for Zanzibar

development up to $2m for the financing of agreed projects [this was never given].Contributions from other donors, particularly UK and the Federal Republic of Germany are important both for funding and to avoid the appearance of a US takeover.

(quoted in Wilson, 1989: 81)

To describe the union between Zanzibar and Tanganyika as an aspect of Nyerere's Pan-Africanism, as some writers have done, is perhaps somewhat naïve. At this point the cold war, like the war on terror today, led to constant interventions by the United States to try to influence and manipulate leaders of African countries, and where they were unable to do so, organize 'regime change'. Nyerere was a survivor, and he was also and always a liberal. As Gora Ebrahim, the South African freedom fighter and leader of the Pan Africanist Congress, who spent many years in Tanzania, told me in an interview in 1988:

> Nyerere had realized that to remain in power given what was happening round him – the overthrow of Nkrumah, for example – he had to consolidate power and at the same time, while remaining dependent on the West, not appear to be the vassal of this or that foreign country.

In this sense, Nyerere was also different from Kenyatta, who prior to independence had a much bigger, more militant profile, and after independence succumbed completely. Nyerere had a much lower profile but developed a progressive cult.

Nyerere had been the moderate leader of TANU, which had negotiated, *not fought*, for independence from the United Kingdom. Later he became the pro-West president of Tanganyika, and as president of the Union between Tanganyika and Zanzibar, he was even more indebted to the West. Given this history, how could he reconcile it with his newly assumed role as a leading East African nationalist and president of an independent, sovereign state? The Colito mutiny helped Nyerere understand that he would have to move away from being the new head of a neocolonial administration. It was in this context that Pan-Africanism was particularly important. It provided a way of rebuilding Nyerere's image. Perhaps this was also one reason why Nyerere would be willing to support liberation movements and make radical statements, even on occasion take on radical positions, but without damaging his relationship with the West.

Even at times of crisis, for example when on January 15, 1965, after the Organization of African Unity (OAU) Liberation Committee revealed that Carlucci and his colleague, US diplomat Robert Gordon, were involved in subversive activities in Tanzania, and Nyerere was forced to expel them, he managed to retain a 'friendly' relationship with the United States. In response to Carlucci and Gordon's expulsions the US authorities not only expelled the Tanzanian consul in the United States but threatened to withdraw aid for various projects. However, as a US Embassy cable commented a few weeks later, 'interesting to note, day-to-day liaison between CIA representative here and GURT [Government of the United Republic of Tanzania] counterparts has been proceeding normally' (quoted in Wilson, 1989: 107).

Karume Signs Away the People's Republic of Zanzibar

The details of who did and who did not know about the plans for the Union, and who did or did not approve, are impossibly difficult to unravel today because of the shortage of concrete documentary evidence, and this is a problem with some recent reconstructions of that period. I have used interviews here where people describe their own actions and thoughts, but have avoided using reconstructions where respondents try to remember not only what other people said but what they now think others thought.

What we do know is that the Union was finally agreed in Babu's absence, that it had been planned and its details worked out in his absence, and that this was deliberate. We also know that he was both shocked and saddened by the impending but apparently irreversible situation which confronted him when he returned from Indonesia (see page 60). He realized that he had no choice but to accept the Union. However, characteristically, in an attempt to find some spark of optimism, he sought positive angles to this otherwise disastrous development, and pointed out to some of his comrades that the union with Tanganyika would at least provide a broader canvas for their struggle for socialism (Babu, personal communication, December 1989).

On April 22 the Articles for the Union were signed by Nyerere and Karume. They sealed a semi-colonial relationship between Zanzibar and Tanganyika. Zanzibar was given limited regional autonomy as far as agriculture, police and courts were concerned, but overall power – over foreign affairs, defence, trade union matters, control of foreign exchange and so on – was held by the centre in Tanganyika.

But remarkably these Articles that determined Union control of the Isles were not ratified by the Zanzibar Revolutionary Council. When they were presented by Karume to the Revolutionary Council, Khamis said that 'due to the seriousness of the matter, the people should be asked to decide through a referendum'. 'Karume replied', Khamis told me, '"If you don't want it, I will return it to him [Nyerere]." Nobody else said anything' (interview with Khamis Ameir, 2009).

Whether Karume himself was aware of the full implications of the Union is not clear. The US documents suggest that he was not. As for the legality of the procedure, Shivji writes:

> All the evidence points to the fact that the purported Zanzibar Law ratifying the Articles of the Union was made and drafted by legal officers of Tanganyika in Tanganyika .... The Revolutionary Council as a whole did not approve the Union. There is no doubt that the Union was 'steamrollered' ... the expatriate legal officers of the Tanganyika Government (who happened in this case also to be friends of Nyerere) simply adopted a legal subterfuge of publishing the Union of Tanganyika and Zanzibar law 1964, which they had made, in the official gazette of the United Republic as a Notice under the signature of Fifoot [one of the expatriate legal officers].
>
> (Shivji, 2008: 93)

Meanwhile, Leonhart cabled Washington passing on a request from Nyerere that to the 'maximum extent, any US public statements on Tangovernment-Zanzibar union be avoided .... Strongly recommend that the line of any public comment should be ... that the project is one for the Tanganyika and Zanzibar people themselves to decide' (quoted in Wilson, 1989: 77). Attwood, the US ambassador to Kenya, added that Nyerere's secretary had told him that 'major power would rest in the centre. The laws of Tanganyika would become supreme throughout .... *He considered this most significant since, he said, the Tanganyika Preventative Detention Act could be used to round up radicals on Zanzibar*' (my emphasis) (quoted in Wilson, 1989: 78).

Early Days of Tanzania – the Mainland

Nyerere's Acolytes 'Look After' the Left

While the legal documents were prepared and signed by British officers, the allocation of posts in the new government on April 27 was also approved by US officials. As Leonhart commented on April 29:

> Nyerere's United Republic has given us the initial political framework with which we can work. Key powers of foreign affairs, finance, army and police are all held at Dar es Salaam and Nyerere's strongest men in charge of each ... [Zanzibaris] hold minor posts and are checked and balanced by Tanganyikans in closely related ministries.
>
> (quoted in Wilson, 1989: 83)

The involvement of British expatriate and US officials was an early warning that constantly seeking approval and advice from the West would become one of the features of the years ahead.

In Tanzania's first cabinet Karume became the first vice president and Rashidi Kawawa the second vice president. The Zanzibaris included Aboud Jumbe, minister of state in the First Vice President's Office; Abdullah Hanga, minister of industry, mines and power; Babu, minister of state in the President's Office and Directorate of Planning; Hassan Nassor Moyo, minister of justice; and Idrisa Abdul Wakil, minister of information and tourism.

As Babu was to comment in an interview in 1988.

> Nyerere used the appointments to weaken the progressive forces. With the assistance of the US ... we were sent to insignificant cabinet posts – for example, in my case, I was put in the Ministry of Economic Planning. But I was not in charge. There were three ministers of state. All three of us were under the president. There was nothing we could do. I could not plan policies or implement them. I did not know what the plan was about – we merely witnessed what others had done. There was a French director of planning. He was in control of planning. The effect of this kind of cabinet was to incapacitate us. We were given big houses and cars but we had no function in Zanzibar and no function on the mainland. [Babu himself rejected these privileges, living modestly, as he had always done, and driving his own car.]

The strict control of almost everyone who could conceivably be considered to be on the left was confirmed by an account of those days by Al Noor Kassum. Kassum, an acolyte of Nyerere, describes how Hanga was 'looked after':

> My Minister was Abdullah Hanga from Zanzibar .... Before the change in portfolio, Mwalimu Nyerere called me in and told me I had a special

role to play in the Ministry. 'You are needed there to help look after Hanga', he said. It soon became clear that Mwalimu was right to be cautious. The Minister had to present his budget to Parliament and after writing his budget speech he sent it to me for my comments. On reading it, I found myself in a dilemma because it was full of radical ideas. So I went to Mwalimu and apprised him of the situation. 'I can change it to some extent but I think it will be very difficult. It really needs to be rewritten,' I told him. Mwalimu then suggested a solution: 'Why don't you tell Mr Hanga that since this is the first time he is presenting this budget, the President himself would like to have a look at his budget speech ....' So, Hanga and I went to State House and sat with Mwalimu. After reading the speech, he told Hanga, 'This is an excellent speech but it needs a little bit of adjustment ....'

(Kassum, 2007: 45)

By the time these 'adjustments' had been made, Al Noor Kassum recollects, 'It was an entirely new speech.'

Despite this situation, Babu continually argued for strategies which he believed would help the development of Tanzania. With a few exceptions (see below) these were blocked. He was continually transferred from one ministry to another while development policies remained, as before, completely in the hands of expatriates.

However, the very presence of Babu and other progressive Zanzibaris in the cabinet helped Nyerere in that they gave Tanzania, and therefore its president, a radical image.

In Pan-African and broader anti-imperialist arenas, Babu was able to continue to strengthen some of his earlier links and relationships in the months after the union. One of these was with the African-American struggle and Malcolm X in particular. He had been in touch with Malcolm soon after the revolution, and met him again in Cairo in July 1964, when both he and Malcolm attended the second summit of the OAU and also the summit of the non-aligned movement. As Babu said in a speech at a conference on Malcolm X: Radical Tradition and a Legacy of Struggle in New York in 1990, Malcolm's 'politics were evolving, he had the vision to see the threat that a united Third World would pose to imperialism'. Malcolm visited Tanzania in the October of that year, by which time they had become close friends. Later that year they spoke together at mass rallies in Harlem. There can be no doubt that Babu was a powerful influence on Malcolm, leading him towards a more explicit anti-imperialist world view.

Malcolm X and Babu
© Keystone/Hulton Archive.

The Tanzania–Zambia rail link, TAZARA

After the expulsion of Carlucci, and despite his continuing warm relationship with the West, Nyerere was anxious that Western aid might become more and more problematic. He became more willing than he had been before to seek aid elsewhere, and he had been impressed by China's approach to Zanzibar. So he decided to visit China, hoping to extend the close relationship between China and Zanzibar built up by Babu to Tanzania as a whole. With this in mind Nyerere asked Babu to go to China two weeks in advance of his own visit.

In an interview in 1988, Babu reminisced on that visit:

> On this earlier trip Premier Zhou Enlai asked me what I thought President Nyerere would like to discuss most. I replied that possibly Nyerere would want to discuss the railway between Tanzania and Zambia. But when Nyerere arrived he did not raise the question of the railway at all. In the end, Zhou Enlai asked him, 'Could you, Mr President, tell us – we heard there is a problem between you and the World Bank regarding the building of the railway, could you brief us?'
>
> (interview with Babu, 1988)

This was the beginning of one of the most ambitious and most

THE UNION WITH TANGANYIKA

On February 10, 1965, a trade agreement and a protocol concerning the exchange of commodities between China and Tanzania were signed by Babu, then Tanzanian minister for trade, and Lin Hai-yun, acting minister for foreign trade for China. Here we see them exchanging documents they had just signed.
Source: Xinhua 330522/0131.

successful transport systems in Africa, the construction of the historic Tanzania–Zambia railway, TAZARA. The rail link's aim was to strengthen Tanzania and Zambia, both of which were Frontline states (states opposing the then apartheid regime of South Africa and supporting the liberation movements). Tanzania would be able to use the rail link to strengthen its economy, expand its infrastructure, and facilitate the development of the countryside. At the same time, Zambia's copper, its major export, would no longer have to pass through the Portuguese-dominated states of Angola and Mozambique or South Africa and Rhodesia, because the country would have an outlet to the sea at Dar es Salaam. As a result Zambia would be able to take a more independent stand on the question of Southern African Liberation movements. The project had been turned down by the World Bank and the US government.

The project was completed in 1975, remarkably some four years

Babu and Vice President Kawawa with heroes of the long march, January 1965
(Photographer unknown.)

in advance of the schedule. It was unique in being a foreign-funded project that actually benefited the people of Tanzania and Zambia.

The Chinese loan was interest free. It was worth US$400 million, one tenth of which was local costs to be paid by Tanzania. But since Tanzania could not afford this sum, the Chinese suggested a financial arrangement whereby they would send goods to Tanzania and the Tanzanian government would sell these goods to raise the money required. In addition, the Chinese kept prices steady even when world prices fell, and Chinese workers in those days did not demand luxuries such as air-conditioned houses.

However, because of Nyerere's expatriate advisers, the full potential of the project was not realized, as Babu commented:

> The Chinese took us seriously; Nyerere never took Tanzanians seriously! At that time he thought Tanzania would remain an agricultural country for ever. If you talked about industry, he thought you were talking about going to the moon. The Chinese trained 3,000 technicians. When they left they told us, why don't you use them and our machinery to build another project? Nyerere said no, because the Chinese are just finishing this project and they should not start another one. What

In the Great Hall of the People, Beijing, 1965. Front row, from left: Marshall Chen Yi, Babu, President Liu Shaoqi, vice president of Tanzania Kawawa, Chairman Mao Zedong, Silo Swai (Tanzania), Premier Zhou Enlai, George Kahama (Tanzania).
(Photographer unknown.)

> would the West say? I said, what does it matter what the West says? What would Tanzanians say? Would they like to get water? Nyerere was not interested.
> (interview with Babu, 1988)

Water accessibility remained extremely poor in many parts of the country. Even today water supply coverage is only 54 per cent, and in remote areas women and children can spend several hours every day collecting water (Wateraid, 2011).

Economic Policies: Differences between Babu and Nyerere

The West had dominated Tanganyika economically without a break since the colonial period. In 1961, when the country became independent, the government asked the US consultancy Arthur D. Little to prepare an industrial strategy for the country. About the same time the World Bank produced an overall strategy for Tanganyika's development.

These reports made sure that the country continued to go down the same path. They emphasized that it must produce more for export and at the same time invite foreign investment and aid – policies, in other words, which were geared to increase profits for multinational companies, not to benefit the people of Tanganyika. These

Babu trying to explain his economic approach to Nyerere
Source: Mohamed Amin/Camerapix.

policies were followed in Tanzania's first Five-Year Plan of 1964, and predictably, they exacerbated the country's economic problems.

In 1967, sensing popular discontent, Nyerere decided on a more populist approach. Abandoning the Five-Year Plan he introduced the Arusha Declaration. The Declaration was heralded as a break with western domination. Babu supported this objective, but his vision of such a break was very different from Nyerere's. In fact the Arusha Declaration illustrated many of the essential political differences between Babu and Nyerere.

Nyerere's 'African Socialism'

For Nyerere, a break with foreign domination was about a return to what he saw as Africa's pre-colonial 'classless' society, which he idealized as based on principles of love between human beings, the right to work and share what was produced equally, and where private ownership was shunned. These principles were sacrosanct because they were thought to have held African society together in precolonial times and had only been undermined as a result of foreign intervention, which brought with it a monetary economy and notions of individual ownership. Nyerere argued from this basis for a return to this mythical past. In rural Tanzania – and most of Tanzania was, and is, rural – this was to be achieved through villageization, or the reorganization of the rural population into planned villages where the peasants would continue to grow cash crops as before.

It also meant, inevitably, the penetration of government and party into the economy and consolidation of economic power at the centre. These policies were presented as 'African socialism'. A key slogan was self-reliance, but in reality it was much more about austerity and control. In fact, the villageization model was in the end not very different from the British colonial model introduced in 1922 and the World Bank policy of 1959, the main difference being that, thanks to Nyerere's moralistic approach to 'self-reliance', it was paid for not with 'foreign money' but at the expense of the people themselves.

While the World Bank had invested an average of $300,000 per village as initial capital for economic and social infrastructure and essential mechanical equipment, under Nyerere the slogan of 'Pesa si msingi wa maendeleo' (money was not the basis of development) meant the villagers had to generate the resources locally and at their own risk. All rural land was brought under this scheme, and by 1967 90 per cent of the rural population had been moved. Its effects were far from positive, as far as the life of ordinary villagers was concerned. While Tanzania had once been self-sufficient in food or in good years even had a surplus, these policies soon resulted in the country being forced to import essential food items.

While imposing villageization, Nyerere also promised welfare services. The problem, as Babu argued, was that there was no money to pay for these services, because in Tanzania (and many other former colonies) the economy depended almost entirely on production through peasant-based agriculture. Whereas in metropolitan countries, production remained in the hands of capitalists and social democratic governments taxed the capitalists to pay for welfare, in Tanzania there was no effective tax base which could pay for welfare on a regular basis. Trying to introduce a welfare state on the basis of this kind of economy would lead to disastrous results, miring the country in poverty and dependence on aid.

Babu's vision of socialism was of course very different. He argued that the view that past African societies were virtuous, and foreign intervention was an evil influence against which everyone must struggle, was an idealistic view of the world, unconnected to reality:

> That the politics and ideology of the past were a concentrated expression of their economics .... They have no relevance to the economics of the present or the economics of the future ... whereas traditionalists talk of equality in poverty, socialists prefer to talk of equality in plenty.
> (Babu, 1981: 58)

In fact poverty was to be one of Nyerere's main legacies. While Tanzania's score on the United Nations Development Programme Human Development Index has increased slightly since 2000, it still ranked 159th out of the 177 participating countries in 2007/08 (ILO, 2011).

Babu's Interpretation of Self-Reliance

In Babu's view, a break with foreign domination (which was after all what the Arusha Declaration claimed to provide) necessitated a change from a colonial economic structure (with its total dependence on cash crops) to a national economy which would focus on production to meet the basic needs of the people: food, clothing and shelter. Self-reliance came, in Babu's view, when a country produced these basic needs through its own efforts and was therefore no longer a victim of the inherent injustices of the world market.

In the period between the Arusha Declaration's announcement and its implementation, he wrote a series of articles entitled 'The Meaning of Self Reliance' in *The Nationalist* newspaper in Dar es Salaam which elaborated on this vision. Here he discussed the Declaration's potential weaknesses and strengths. He pointed out that without a Programme of Action the objectives of the Declaration would not be achieved (Babu, 1967).

Such a programme, he wrote, must reduce unproductive aspects of government machinery, must work for national unity and develop seven key areas – agriculture, animal husbandry and fishing; industrial production; mineral resources; communications; public health; education; and rural housing.

Investment in agriculture would include modernizing food production through, for example, large state farms along river belts, flood control and irrigation. As he wrote later, if this had been done 'Tanzania would have strengthened its position as the food-surplus producing country that it used to be. Natural hazards, floods or droughts would have had very limited damaging effects' (Babu, [1981] 2002: 22).

He emphasized that investment in industry would have included the exploitation of Tanzania's coal and iron ore resources and developing industrial complexes, providing skills and employment. Tanzania would then have been able to build tractors, trucks, water-pumping machines, construction machinery, machine tools, and meet many of its other basic development needs.

Sadly for Tanzania, the policies that Babu proposed and consistently argued for at the TANU Central Committee were ignored. In February 1972, Nyerere reshuffled the Cabinet and dropped a number of the most experienced ministers, including Babu. They were replaced by inexperienced men who were uncritically loyal to Nyerere, who described them as *waumini* (religious believers).

After this change, people's experiences of villageization quickly became far more harsh and oppressive, and what had been launched as a voluntary programme soon became compulsory. In November 1973, Nyerere declared that 'To live in villages is an order!' (quoted in Havnevik, 1993: 205). People who refused to move had their houses destroyed and were forcibly evicted before being transported in military or prison trucks. The rural population was moved at an incredible pace and without regard to the consequences for agriculture, ecology or even planning. In fact, agricultural production suffered, peasants were in many areas reduced to subsistence farming, and food shortages hit the country.

Ironically, throughout the 1970s, the people who had been forced to move from the land on which they had lived for generations and those struggling to survive in the new schemes moved away from the countryside and flocked to cities, seeking employment but often not finding anything but the most casual kinds. This type of urbanization increased faster in Tanzania than almost anywhere else in the world (O'Connor, 1988).

Nationalization of the Wholesale Trade

Another major difference in economic policy between Nyerere and Babu concerned wholesale trade. In 1971, Nyerere decided to nationalize wholesale trade (which was mainly in the hands of Asian families).

No reason was given for the implementation of this policy except that it came under a vague notion of 'socialism'. Babu opposed it, arguing at length that such nationalization would raise the cost of distribution and dislocate the business system; that the Tanzanian economy at that point needed to develop productive forces[1] by integrating both private and government resources; and that 'the state should not become a seller of bread and butter', it 'should be creating new areas of development, either large scale farming or industries. This is where government resources should go instead of tying them to the distributive trade' (quoted in Wilson, 1989: 135).

The very next day the government took the decision to nationalize commerce. Babu was bypassed by a special task force appointed by Nyerere and headed by his principal secretary.

CHAPTER FIVE

Karume's Despotic Rule

Having got rid of Babu and others whom he saw as potential threats from Zanzibar after the Union, Karume also removed almost all other educated members of the Revolutionary Council, and began to rule the islands as his personal fiefdom.

In February 1965 laws were passed which indefinitely postponed the convening of a Constituent Assembly. The next eight years were a time of unprecedented bloodshed and terror, in the course of which the rule of law was ignored, opponents were brutally murdered, sexual assault and forced marriages were widespread, trade unions and all people's organizations were banned, and movement in and out of Zanzibar was strictly controlled. The ASP and the Zanzibar state were made indistinguishable. In addition, since Karume exercised total power without any form of accountability, the islands were opened to looting by Karume's family.

As Tahir Qazi writes, analysing Mubarak's Egypt:

> autocracy fosters a few elites and creates a social pyramid where power, wealth and opportunities are concentrated at the top ... better termed a Pyramid of Injustice. The autocratic rulers with the help of their foreign sponsors create dependent states .... This has important ramifications for the local population ... for overt and covert reasons.
> (Qazi, 2011)

This is equally true of Zanzibar in the post-Union years.

Economically, socially and politically, Zanzibar experienced its worst years of the century. The population dwindled as middle-class people, or those with skills, found ways of fleeing the islands.

If Karume had indeed been a Zanzibari nationalist, as many have claimed, would he have destroyed the very fabric of Zanzibari society?

Karume Hands Military Power to his Henchmen

Aware that he might need the army to safeguard his position, Karume reorganized it to hand control to his most trusted henchmen. In the period immediately after the revolution, the men from the Umma cadres who had been to Cuba had worked hard to establish the Zanzibar army, the People's Liberation Army (PLA). But as Karume's dictatorial powers grew, he began to regard them as a threat. As Shaaban told me, 'Karume wanted us to be out of the way. So in July 1964, 18 of us who had trained in Cuba were sent to the Soviet Union for one year' (interview with Shaaban, 2009).

When they returned in 1965, they found out that they would not be allowed to return to Zanzibar. As Hamed Hilal told me:

> It was funny how we found out about this .... When we arrived from Moscow we had been put in a hotel in Dar es Salaam. The next day we were busy at Army headquarters. We had no time to connect with Babu or other comrades. But to our surprise at around 8 pm when we came down to the lounge, outside on the verandah we saw Babu, Badawi and Saleh Saadalla .... It was Badawi who revealed that we were not wanted in Zanzibar. This was confirmed to us when we went to Zanzibar for a two-week holiday and paid a courtesy call to Karume at State House. He told us that we must either go to embassies as military attachés or go to the mainland and work. We chose the latter because we wanted to remain in the army as this was our profession.
>
> (interview with Hamed Hilal, 2011)

They were split into two groups, one sent to Tabora and the other to Nachingwea army camps. Hamed continued:

> It was a calculated move. Although it was normal for military officers to be posted in different units when they finished their courses, in our case the main aim was to observe and follow our activities and also to prevent communications between us and other ex-Umma members. Army intelligence officers were given the job of surveillance on us. They reported about our activities to headquarters who in turn reported to Zanzibar.
>
> (interview with Hamed Hilal, 2011)

The Nachingwea group of ex-Umma cadres became very friendly with fellow officers, including the intelligence officers, and won their trust. Eventually the intelligence officers told them that they were actually there to observe and report on them. After a few months these security men realized that there was nothing suspicious to report and the surveillance was abandoned. But the ex-Umma members remained in these posts for the next two years. After that, as Hamed told me, 'some of us were transferred to Dar. There we met again and were with Babu almost every weekend.'[1]

This was the period when, as Shaaban told me, Karume reorganized the army with Committee of Fourteen men like Seif Bakari and Abdalla Natepe, and Yusuf Himid, who was made commander. (Ali Mahfoudh, who had been commander of the PLA, was also moved to the mainland a few months later and sent to the Tanzania-Mozambique border to help train Mozambican freedom fighters.) Shaaban told me:

> At that time there was still a Zanzibar army, but there were suggestions that it should be integrated with the Tanganyikan army and people in Zanzibar did not know how to resist .... The PLA was disbanded in 1966. There was a vacuum and then came the period of killings .... Seif Bakari and the Committee of Fourteen killed any number of people and many others disappeared – even today no one knows what happened to them. And there was a continuous process of removing all progressive people from the army and from the government in Zanzibar.
> (interview with Shaaban Salim, 2009)

Days of Violence and Tyranny

At this time the Committee of Fourteen were being treated as national heroes by those in power in Zanzibar and also in Tanzania as a whole. On January 12, 1965, the first anniversary of the revolution, *The Nationalist*, the Dar es Salaam newspaper, for example, carried photographs of them in a so-called 'Gallery of the 14'– men 'delegated and led by Abeid Amani Karume, the first Vice President of the United Republic of Tanzania to prepare the groundwork for the Rising which ended the rule of the Sultan'.

These men could now act with impunity, kill, imprison and torture whoever they wanted. Indefinite detention, torture and summary execution became common. People were killed for criticizing the regime or because they were perceived as critics, or else to settle scores, and sometimes for no identifiable reason at all, (interviews with Shaaban Salim and Khamis Ameir, 2009). Torture chambers were established all over Zanzibar island, in which innocent men and women were subjected to the most inhuman cruelty. The most notorious of these chambers was the *kwa bwamkwe*, as it was popularly known. It was in Zanzibar central prison in Kiinuwamiguu (*Zanzibar Election Watch*, 2005: 3).

Under Karume's leadership the Committee of Fourteen now consolidated around themselves other groups of violent men, including many who had been trained as torturers by the East German Stasi. Men who carried out the torture were organized into groups, among which was the notorious Group Number Eight. The Zanzibar Committee for Democracy named many of them in its monthly newspaper as part of *Zanzibar Election Watch* (2005: 3), and noted also that several of them, including the men who had tortured Hashil and Hamed, had held important posts in the Tanzanian diplomatic and intelligence services and the cabinet.

In 1967 the Karume clique began to target the progressive members of the ASP one by one. Forced confessions implicating these men and others were wrung out of people indiscriminately arrested by the regime. In one such instance, Captain Ahmada, a member of the Umma Party, was coerced into implicating 19 people – many of whom had made criticisms of the regime – in an entirely fictitious anti-Karume plot. (It was Ahmada and Humud Mohamed, also a Umma cadre, who would assassinate Karume in 1972.)

The ASP members implicated were charged and publicly denounced, and then imprisoned and executed without even the pretence of a trial. Abdulaziz Twala, who was finance minister and had been in the trade union movement, was killed, and so was Saleh Sadalla. In 1968 Hanga and Othman Shariff too were brutally murdered. As Hanga's wife Lily Golden, a Russian African-American historian and political activist, learned through access to secret documents, Hanga had been shot at close range and his mutilated body dumped in the Indian Ocean (Free Library, 2009).

As Shaaban recollected, 'the period also saw a continuous sacking and imprisonment of progressives and it was at this time that Badaawi and Ali Sultan were both dismissed'. It was also in this period that the ASP leadership, threatened by the genuine mass support Babu enjoyed on the islands, demanded that he be dismissed from his post by Nyerere and sent back to Zanzibar as Hanga had been earlier. But Nyerere, knowing perhaps what would be in store, refused at this stage.

In 1969, to facilitate the elimination of all critics, Karume and his henchmen made some fundamental changes to the judicial system. Lower courts were abolished and replaced by People's Courts. These were presided over by three people, a chairman and two others appointed by the president, who served 'during the pleasure of the President'. These judges were almost without exception semi-literate, with no knowledge of the law or legal procedures. Like most of Karume's right-wing clique, however, they were vindictive men who ruled on cases with arbitrary cruelty. They decided court procedure completely unchallenged, since no advocates were allowed to appear. As Khamis recalled, 'There were so many arrests and disappearances. They would put you inside. They would say, "See those people walking outside? They are good people. You are here because you are guilty."' The People's Courts remained the mainstay of the legal system till the 1980s (interview with Khamis Ameir, 2009).

Khamis recollected that he was the only one of the ex-Umma members left in the Revolutionary Council:

> There were so many occasions when they tried to get rid of me. There was the incident about workers' wages, then the incident about the Vietnam war, and one time Karume said 'We have information that you give jobs to Arabs.' Then someone in his office stood up for me and said, 'No, he is not the person...'. Then the last thing was, 'You are an Arab – of mixed blood. Who are you mixed with?' I looked at him and said, 'From your tribe.' Karume was from Malawi, and my grandmother was from Malawi. I told him that. He looked at me, then he changed the subject. After that all the problems ended. Every time there was a committee formed, he would say, 'Put Khamis on!' Sometimes I would say, 'I can't be on this committee, they are robbing the government.' He would insist, 'Stay there!'
>
> (interview with Khamis, 2009)

For the majority of the people of Zanzibar, one of the worst aspects of Karume's rule was the extreme food shortage created by his policies. The economy had not been diversified or modernized. It remained tied to the production of cloves for export, and vulnerable to the ups and downs of the world market. But to make things far worse, the income received from sale of cloves was hoarded, so that the people of Zanzibar suffered even when clove prices were high. The money was stashed away in the London branch of the Moscow Narodny Bank, while a ban was imposed on the importation of food.

By 1972, people's sufferings were so great that, as Chase writes:

> the long-standing latent opposition to ASP rule was beginning to assume a mass, public character for the first time since the 1967 anti-Karume 'plot'. In response to this the Karume clique prepared the way for another purge of potentially dissident elements, especially those whose historical role made them likely candidates for mass support.
>
> (Chase, 1976: 19)

In February of that year, Karume sent a high-level delegation to Dar es Salaam to demand the extradition of Babu and other ex-Umma Party members who were on the mainland. This demand appeared to be motivated by the fact that as Karume's grip on Zanzibar grew more tyrannical, Babu had emerged as the major critic of the ASP regime.

This time too Nyerere refused to extradite Babu. But he decided to compromise by dismissing Babu from his post. The manner of the dismissal suggests that Nyerere wanted to collaborate with Karume in an attempt to publicly humiliate Babu. He asked him for no apparent reason to deputize for the foreign minister, John Malecella, and lead a Tanzanian delegation to the OAU Council of Ministers. When Babu was out of the country attending this meeting, he was abruptly and publicly dismissed from his post as minister of economic affairs and development planning (Babu, 1996: 331).

Karume's Assassination and its Aftermath

It was in this atmosphere of intrigue at the highest level of the government, of unprecedented repression in Zanzibar and mounting public anger, that Karume was assassinated on April 7, 1972. The two men who assassinated Karume were both ex-Umma members, Lt Humud Mohamed, whose bullets actually killed Karume, and Captain Ahmada. Each of them had their personal reasons for assassinating Karume. Humud's father had been murdered in prison, allegedly on Karume's orders, and Ahmada had suffered torture by the Karume clique which had forced him to make false allegations. Humud and Ahmada, and two other men said to have been involved in the assassination, were killed by the police following Karume's death.

While most Zanzibaris must have rejoiced at least in private about

Karume's death, it led to a situation where Karume's most trusted and most violent henchmen, led by Seif Bakari, were the only group with power in the islands.

Eventually Aboud Jumbe was chosen as the next president of Zanzibar. He was a compromise candidate, chosen partly because he was acceptable to the Bakari clique and partly because he was less intensely hated by the masses than many others who had been part of Karume's regime. One of the few educated men tolerated by Karume, he was remarkably skilful at ignoring even the most blatant injustice and cruelty. He now turned this skill to making the necessary compromises and concessions to the clique. This also enabled him to strengthen his position, and retain, and ultimately consolidate, his power.

The Seif Bakari clique asserted their power immediately after the assassination, and 1,100 people were arrested and thrown into prison in the next few days. They were, by and large, ex-Umma Party members and supporters, and ASP members – people who were thought to have been critical of the Karume regime and therefore considered political opponents of the clique.

The events from this point till the beginning of the so-called Treason Trial fall into four major overlapping periods. The first covers the arrest and interrogation of the detainees in Zanzibar and their 'confessions' under severe torture and in some cases under pain of death. Second is the fabrication of a huge plot on the basis of these 'confessions'. The aim of this 'plot', supposedly led by Babu and the Umma Party, was claimed to be to kill Karume and then seize power in the islands. Third, while the 'confessions' were being wrung out and the 'plot' concocted, there were the arrests of Babu and other ex-Umma members on the mainland. Finally came the interrogation of these men, which included torture for two of them, Hashil Seif Hashil and Hamed Hilal (interview with Hamed Hilal, 2011).

Khamis was arrested on April 18, 1972, the last Umma cadre to be arrested in Zanzibar in the immediate aftermath of the assassination. He had been the only one left on the Revolutionary Council, and as he told me 'only the president could sign for someone from the Revolutionary Council to be arrested. So, soon after Jumbe became president, I was arrested and put in prison. And I found the rest of my comrades there!' (interview with Khamis Ameir, 2009).

On his arrival in prison Khamis also saw the torturers waiting. They were to carry out such inhuman torture that three people – Mussa Abdalla Ali, popularly known as 'Meki', Lt Ali Othman and Abbass Mohamed, all of them ex-Umma Party members – died even before the trial started. Others, among them Saleh Ali and Muhammed Saghir, were to die soon afterwards. The interrogation room, according to one defendant, resembled 'an abattoir splashed with human blood' (Chase, 1976: 24). Other tortures perpetrated included sexual violence, being forced to stand buried up to the neck in sand or mud, psychological violence: snakes with fangs removed would be placed in the cell, bullets would be sprayed around the detainee, and hanging would be simulated with the rope adjusted so as not to kill (interview with Khamis Ameir, 2009).

On various occasions in 1972, 'Dourado [attorney general Wolfgang Dourado, who was the prosecutor] would come to the interrogation room', Khamis told me, 'read the statements and then say, "You have to extract more from this man", i.e. more torture. In court he said, "They just had their arms twisted, that is all."' In fact, Dourado's statement on this subject is worth quoting in full. It reveals an approach which has some interesting contemporary parallels in the trials of those accused under UK and US terrorism laws. Here too the use of evidence obtained under torture is commonplace:

> During the trial those who admitted guilt in their statement retracted them. They contended that the statements were improperly obtained and were therefore not voluntary statements. Because of the conditions in which these statements were taken they were forced to admit guilt and concoct lies, and in other cases investigating officers added to their statements in order to strengthen the case against them. The question that firstly arises is, are these statements admissible in law? The short answer to this question is that while they would be inadmissible in some systems of law, our system has no bar to the admissibility of such statements. Your honour will observe that I am conceding that some form of arm twisting was adopted in order to obtain these statements.
>
> (Chase, 1976: 24)

Arrests, Incarceration and Torture on the Mainland

After nearly a year of relentless interrogation under torture of those imprisoned, the authorities finally obtained the 'confessions' they sought. Well before this, in fact only six days after the assassination, all the ex-Umma cadres living on the mainland, including Babu, had been arrested and detained.

Babu was at the time of his arrest already aware that he was in danger, because at Karume's funeral on April 10, there had been a chilling indication of what was to come. Edington Kisai, the commissioner of police, told Mohammed Sahnun, the Algerian deputy general-secretary of the OAU who had come to attend the funeral, 'We are going to get Babu, alive or dead' (Babu, 1975: 1). Sahnun was shocked, and on arrival in Dar es Salaam on his way back to Algeria, he sent a message to Babu telling him of this sinister threat. Babu immediately informed the vice president, Rashid Kawawa, asking him to take appropriate measures. He also asked to see Nyerere, but his request, Babu recalled, was refused with utmost rudeness (Babu, 1975: 2).

The arrest which Babu had been forewarned about was violent. As he wrote in a letter to the UN Commission on Human Rights:

> On 13 April, at 3 AM in the morning, my house was surrounded by the para-military police, armed to the teeth, and in typical Gestapo tradition they banged on my door in the name of law and order, arrested and handcuffed me, with loaded sub-machine guns pointed at my head. ... Although I was shown no arrest order or search warrant, and much less told what all this brute force was in aid of, yet a gang of secret police walked in along with the armed gendarmes, and started ransacking my house and taking anything they thought they wanted .... While they continued ransacking my house they ordered me out ... leaving my terrified family behind. I had no choice. They had already handcuffed me so they dragged me out of the house, helter-skelter, and shoved me into a waiting van in which were additional armed gendarmes.
>
> (Babu, 1975: 2)

He was taken to Ukonga prison, where he spent two weeks in isolation before being transferred in chains, via Dodoma prison, to the Tabora prison, where he was thrown into the 'condemned cells' next to the execution chamber. Here he spent the next ten months, seven of them in solitary confinement. In this whole period he was never told the reasons for his detention, although under the Preventative Detention Act he had this right, if few others, since this colonial law (which is still on the statute books in Tanzania) deprives those imprisoned under it of almost all civil rights.

All other ex-Umma Party cadres on the mainland were also arrested on the same day. Hamed Hilal, who was in Dar es Salaam, was arrested along with his wife Fatma. They were taken to Keko prison, where other Zanzibari army officers working in the mainland were already incarcerated. Hamed told me:

> There were four Zanzibari women who were arrested in this period. Humud's wife, Fathiya Humud, was released three months later because of pregnancy, and the rest including my wife were released after two years. My wife went back to the army hospital where she used to work but was told that 'for security reasons' she could not be re-employed. She somehow managed to find work in a private clinic until she went to Dubai with our children and her mother who had been looking after them while she was inside. It was only after I was released that I saw my wife when she came to see me for one month.
> (interview with Hamed Hilal, 2011)

The incarceration of these women, who could not conceivably have had any connection to the assassination, demonstrated once more both the Zanzibar government's misogyny and its hatred of 'Arabs'. This cruel and blatant abuse of human rights, in which women like Fatma Hilal and Fathiya Humud were sentenced for their husband's actions (Fathiya being incarcerated even though she was pregnant and her husband was dead) was allowed to pass without even a word of censure by Nyerere. His remark in 1969 (made in discussing the Biafran war) that 'If we do not learn to criticize injustice within our continent, we will soon be tolerating fascism in Africa, as long as it is practised by African governments against African people' (Pomerance, 1982) was proving to be an exercise in self-parody.

There was an attempt to keep all these arrests secret, because when questioned by foreign correspondents, the minister of the interior who had carried out the arrests categorically denied that Babu had been arrested at all (Babu, 1975: 2). Clearly Nyerere was embarrassed, but as was so often the case, he did nothing, and through his inaction effectively collaborated in these abuses.

Babu's wife Ashura and their children were allowed to visit him in Tabora, although the cost and time involved in travelling there prevented them from going more than a few times. Through them he learned of the hundreds of others arrested in Zanzibar and of reports of horrific tortures.

In March 1973, all the Umma cadres including Babu were transferred to the notorious Ukonga maximum security prison on the outskirts of Dar es Salaam. They were placed once again in the condemned cells. Conditions in Ukonga were abysmal, and the treatment meted out to Babu, a former minister, and his comrades, some of them senior army officers, was no different from that given to ordinary criminals. Perhaps if they had been accused of systematically impoverishing the country they would have been treated better, and Ukonga would have been revamped with special VIP rooms, as it was in 2008 in preparation for the prosecutions of ex-ministers and government servants accused of swindling gigantic sums (*Jamiiforums*, 2008).

It was around this time that Jumbe and Hasan Nassor Moyo, the Zanzibar minister of state, arrived on the mainland and approached Nyerere to allow Zanzibari interrogators to carry out investigations on the mainland. Hashil Seif Hashil described these 'investigations' in a talk given to the Sixth Arab-European Human Rights meeting in Berlin on May 12, 2011:

> I was picked up from my prison cell by a group of torturers from Zanzibar. I was blindfolded and handcuffed. After a while I realized that I was not alone. [Hamed Hilal had also been picked up from Keko prison.]
>
> They took us from prison at about 10 pm in the evening to a house somewhere in Dar es-Salaam where they used to torture people. After we arrived they put us in separate rooms.
>
> The walls were covered with human blood. There were about eight torturers. They used electric wires, guava tree and bamboo canes to beat us with .... The fury on our torturers' faces reminded me of injured animals missed by a hunter's bullet. They insisted that it was me who killed the vice president Karume, in order to overthrow the legitimate government of ASP.
>
> (transcript of talk at the Sixth Arab-European Human Rights meeting, Berlin, May 12, 2011)

He was shown photographs of detainees from Zanzibar, many of whom under torture had implicated him. Later both he and Hamed were asked to sign a confession, and when they refused the torture started again:

> one by one each of the torturers took turns to beat me with electric wires until I could not stand it any longer and I fell down unconscious, with blood oozing from my body. They kept saying, 'you will know what happened to *kanga* (a bird) which lost its feathers'. They repeated

those words while torturing me, the rest you can imagine. While they were torturing me, I felt like I was submerged under fire. They asked me to sit on a chair, stripped off my shirt so my stomach was bare and started to torture me till I was unconscious and fell on the floor.
(transcript of talk at the Sixth Arab-European Human Rights meeting, Berlin, May 12, 2011)

Hashil was threatened with rape, and although these torturers did not carry this out, or subject him to other sexual violence, male rape was a feature of the Zanzibar government's torture and intimidation both in this phase and later. In 2001, for example, Napoli and Saleh describe a sustained campaign of attacks on opposition activists during which sexual violence was used against both men and women in Pemba (Napoli and Saleh, 2005: 167).

However, the brutality of the men sent by the Zanzibar government to torture Hashil was witnessed by their counterparts on the mainland, and even these hardened security officers and interrogators from Dar es Salaam were shocked by what they saw. They informed the Tanzania director of intelligence, and he in turn called Nyerere and gave him a full description of these events, emphasizing that if this torture was not stopped the victims could well die.

Nyerere gave orders that the torture should stop. Having tried to hide the fact of their imprisonment from the foreign media and diplomats, he was appalled at the prospect of having to explain away the deaths of these ex-Umma cadres. He gave orders also for trained investigators to interrogate the detainees from then on. He also ordered that the torturers be arrested and punished. They were in fact locked up, but according to Hashil, 'After a few weeks, they were released, while I was put back in prison where I spent six years of my life' (interview with Hashil Seif, 2012).

Clearly the intention of the Zanzibar government had been to incarcerate these men for life. As Hamed told me:

In all this time till the trial finished we were never told the reasons of our arrest. When Hasan Nassor Moyo came to visit Dodoma prison as minister of home affairs, we asked him why we were imprisoned. He told us, 'Don't you know the reason? You will rot here forever.'
(interview with Hamed, 2011)

The interrogations continued, but the trained investigators from the mainland found nothing incriminating. Prior to the assassination, the defendants had gone fishing. There were no weapons on board their boat – only food! Everything pointed to their innocence, but that was irrelevant, because what those in power had in mind was a show trial to demonize the accused and to demonstrate that from now on all dissent would be brutally crushed.

CHAPTER SIX

Trial in Zanzibar's Kangaroo Court

While interrogations and tortures were being carried out on the mainland, in Zanzibar the ground had been prepared for a show trial of the left to be held in the People's Courts. Developments a few months earlier had prepared the media and the people of Zanzibar for it. The first ASP Conference in ten years, held in December 1972 under the leadership of Jumbe, had all but proclaimed that this would be the case. In the presence of Nyerere and other dignitaries from TANU, four resolutions had been passed, each one confirming a racially vindictive and right-wing agenda. The first two ruled that all former ZNP, ZPPP and Umma Party members would be banned from holding positions in the government of the Isles or from becoming full members of the ASP. The third barred non-ASP members from serving in the police and army, and the last called for the trial and public execution of all those found guilty in the alleged anti-Karume conspiracy.

The Trial

The trial itself began on May 5, 1973, about a year after the mass arrests. Of those tried, 81 were charged with treason, including 18 mainland detainees. While Jumbe tried to have these 18, including Babu, extradited to Zanzibar, Nyerere continued to refuse, possibly because he felt that it might lead to international outrage. As a result these men were tried in absentia. Nyerere did nothing to prevent what was not only a grave miscarriage of justice but an illegal act, since under Tanzanian law trials in absentia were not allowed, and because moreover trials in absentia presuppose that the accused have refused to appear in court.

Nyerere's actions and inaction in this case and his failure to stand up for innocent people, as with his dealings with the British and Americans before the Union, underlined his lack of courage and his inability to take a principled stand against right-wing pressure.

The trial took place in the People's Courts of Zanzibar. Khamis recollected:

> The judge was a seller of fish. He didn't know about the law. He used to tell us in court, 'You are like fish in my basket, I can take the one I want and leave the one I don't want.' He used to say that in court! Those were the 'people's judges' – they were supposed to look at things from the Afro Shirazi point of view.
>
> (interview with Khamis Ameir, 2009)

For those who were tried in absentia, the trial was in fact an exercise in character assassination through a reiteration of concocted stories. It lasted for almost a year, and was publicized in all the national newspapers. As Babu wrote to the chair of the United Nation Commission on Human Rights:

> While we were deprived of defending ourselves or even being present at the trial ... our names were slandered and publicly vilified, being called all sorts of names the foul mouth of the prosecution could spit out, and all this time we were silenced behind prison walls.
>
> (Babu, 1975: 5)

The accused men's families were already suffering acutely. In almost every case they faced economic deprivation with their main wage earners incarcerated. Now as the trial dragged on, these families faced further humiliation and pain.

The 'evidence' that Wolfgang Dourado, the prosecutor, presented against those accused speaks for itself. It consisted of statements from nine men who had pleaded guilty and been sentenced to death, and were awaiting the response to a mercy petition. These men had been told that a guilty plea would ensure a lighter sentence, though this proved to be untrue. Their statements implicated all but six of the rest of the defendants. In addition to these statements there were self-confessions (all of which were retracted) from all the defendants arrested on the Isles and six others against whom there was never any other evidence produced. In every case this 'evidence' was extracted under torture.

Also taken as 'evidence' were the defendants' personal and political links with Babu, which they never denied. Finally there was circumstantial evidence about the whereabouts of Babu and other defendants at the time of the assassination:

> [By] accepting the testimony of the nine, and the unanimously retracted confessions of the other defendants, the prosecution were only able to establish the facts, well-known to anyone faintly familiar with Tanzanian/Zanzibari affairs, that Babu was severely critical of the ASP's administration of Zanzibar, that he and several other defendants were avowed Communists, and that they had all met socially with one another on numerous occasions.
>
> (Chase, 1976: 25)

Khamis told me that he was asked by Prosecutor Dourado "'Do you know that Marx said, religion was the opium of the people?" I asked him, "Am I accused of being a Marxist or of killing the president?" He wanted to appease the Americans.'

As for Babu, his communist principles dominated the trial. He was cast in Dourado's presentations as the devil incarnate. Dourado commented, for example:

> For a proper understanding of the prosecution case it is necessary to study the character of the villain of the piece, Abdulrahman Mohamed Babu. As alleged by the prosecution, he has been the guiding force behind the plot .... It was he who conceived the plot to overthrow the Government of the Afro-Shirazi Party as long back as 1968. He was the master mind and arch-instigator of the plot.
>
> ... What policy did Babu and his comrades wish to introduce in Zanzibar? The weight of evidence indicates that they were after scientific socialism. Witnesses like Miraji Mpatani, Qullatein Badawi and co-accused Ali Sultan (who appear to understand their politics) stated that scientific socialism was communism ... if one understands Babu he is not the type of person to respect the wishes of the masses. As leader of the Umma Party, he spoke of a Vanguard party. What this in fact means is that a bunch of tyrants posing as scientific socialists would impose their will on the masses.
>
> (Chase, 1976: 25–7)

Quite apart from the intense anti-communist atmosphere of the trial, it was full of absurd inconsistencies. At the end Dourado was asking the court to believe a ridiculous story which even the most gullible would find hard to swallow:

> [that the so-called plot] masterminded by one of the major political leaders of the 1964 revolution (Babu), involving military figures of the armed insurrection in 1964, as well as the former Chief of Operations of the Tanzanian army (Mahfoudh), and carefully planned over a four year period, consisted of sending one man (Ahmada) to seize control of Bavuai Camp, Army Headquarters, and the Army Radio School, one man (Dugheshi) to … capture Karume, take him to the Radio station and … [then] … take over State House … one man (Baramia) to control ASP Youth League Headquarters, i.e. armed centre of command of Karume's major internal security figure, Seif Bakari; and evidently having a spare man available – left one man (Ameir) to deal with any counter attack … most of the defendants allegedly assigned key military tasks were not members of the Zanzibari Army.
>
> (Chase, 1976: 29)

For the judges, however, this absurd fabrication was enough. Of the 18 mainland detainees 14 were found guilty, and so were 40 of those detained in Zanzibar. Death sentences were handed out without restraint.

Amnesty International, which carried out a powerful campaign to release the prisoners – adopting Babu as a prisoner of conscience – reported in a document on the death penalty in Tanzania (which concentrated on the period 1973–6, although also touching on 1977) that in all:

> 42 death penalties had been imposed by the People's Court. Thirteen of these sentences were imposed in absentia on people detained on the mainland but not handed over to the Zanzibar authorities because the Tanzanian authorities considered that the defendants would not receive a fair trial.
>
> (Amnesty International, 1979: 1)

Hamed told me that:

> one or two months after the kangaroo court trial in Zanzibar was over and sentences were passed, we were moved to other prisons – some of us, Salim Saleh, Shaaban and Badru Said, Haji Othmana and myself, were moved to Dudoma; Ahmed Tony and Tahir Ali were sent to Tabora; and Amour and Abdulla Juma were sent to Mbeya; Suleiman Sisi to Mwanza; and Hashil was sent to Tanga. Babu and Ali Mahfoudh remained at Ukonga all through. Ali Yusuf was released a few months after the trial.
>
> (interview with Hamed Hillal, 2011)

The Long Years in Prison

The Umma cadres were now faced with an apparently endless sentence. Prisoners, particularly those in Zanzibar, were made to suffer in a variety of ways. The food they were given, for example, was not only of the poorest quality but was often deliberately contaminated with low-level poisons. Cassava would be boiled in a container which had been used for diesel oil and then left to stand before it was handed out. At times it would contain toxic cassava leaves, or there would be a porridge made of rotten maize and beans with worms in them. Sanitary conditions were appalling: in the cells there was only a small hole as a toilet to be used by eight or nine people. 'Some of our comrades died', Khamis told me, 'from lack of treatment of wounds from torture or from dysentery …. We went on hunger strike and eventually they agreed to let our people bring soap and tooth paste and better food.' These years after the trial took their toll on the families and loved ones of the ex-Umma cadres. 'Our families – most were broken', Khamis told me. His son was brought to prison when he himself was incarcerated there:

> My son was 17, his mother couldn't control him. They put him in prison with a number of other young people. We used to share our food with them. Then they stopped allowing that. Eventually my son was released. He was put in a school for delinquents which the government had opened. He was there almost two years. When I got out he was out also. He went to Burundi and soon after that he died – hit by a bus in Dar es Salaam. I collected the body from the mortuary …. All this was a direct or indirect result of government actions. Maybe the plan was that we should die in prison. They went to our wives and said, 'Go to your husband in prison and say you want a divorce. He is not going to be out.' It was like a task they gave – you had to sign the letter granting a divorce.
>
> (interview with Khamis, 2009)

Mingling with the other prisoners, they witnessed the wide range of individuals affected by the mindless repression of the Tanzanian state. Khamis told me

> We had a young man from Malawi. They picked him just because he was a Comorian. He was in prison for a long time with me. Sometimes people were picked up out of malice, sometimes for ideological reasons, sometimes just for a whim.
>
> (interview with Khamis, 2009)

On the mainland, Babu and his comrades came across groups of liberation fighters from Frelimo, the People's Movement for the Liberation of Angola (MPLA), the Zimbabwe African People's Union (ZAPU), the African National Congress (ANC), the Pan Africanist Congress (PAC) and the South West Africa People's Organisation (SWAPO), and Lumumbaists and Muleleists from Zaire – all imprisoned on the orders of their leaders. They included Andreas Schipanga, former information secretary of SWAPO, Andreas Nuukwawo, a former youth league activist who had been detained and flogged in Namibia, and nine other ex-members of SWAPO detained for 'threatening the security of Tanzania' (Amnesty International, 1978: 3). They had been jailed by the leaders of their movements to which Tanzania, as the base of the OAU Liberation Committee, was playing host. They and the ex-members of the ANC, PAC and ZAPU were serving sentences of up to seven years.

Babu was determined not to allow the long years in prison to break his spirit. As his many prison notebooks testify, he undertook a study of Marxist philosophy, reflecting on the 'dualism of moral strength and weakness, happiness and sorrow, right and wrong, their relative interpretation and the system of justice based on promoting one and suppressing the other' (Babu, 1996: 332). He also organized classes in Marxist theory and basic political economy for the 119 or so political prisoners (most of them unconnected to the Zanzibar trial) who were in Ukonga while he was there. It was out of the discussions provoked by these lectures that his seminal book *African Socialism or Socialist Africa* took shape. It was a critique of the Tanzanian experience in the post-independence era, and argued for a democratic mass-based people-led socialism based on the reality of Africa. It was to appear in 1981 published by Zed Press, and became one of the most influential books for young progressive Africans of the 1980s and 1990s.

The Campaign for the Release of Babu and All Political Prisoners

In 1975, by which time the defendants had been in prison more than three years, during which death and torture had occurred and some of them had been in solitary confinement for up to a year, 18 of the 42 death sentences were commuted on appeal to the High Court of Zanzibar. After two more years, on February 9, 1977, the Supreme Council of the Afro-Shirazi Party announced the result of the final judicial appeal in the Zanzibar Treason Trial. Seven death sentences were confirmed (four of them in absentia on mainland detainees) and 17 were commuted to 30 or 35-year sentences, six of them in absentia. The remaining death sentences awaited review by the chair of the Revolutionary Council, Aboud Jumbe.

However, as Amnesty International noted, 'No result had been announced by the end of 1977' (Amnesty International, 1979) The four sentenced to death on the mainland were Babu, Ali Mahfoudh, Tahir Ali and Hamed Hilal.

Meanwhile a campaign for the release of the treason trial defendants was building internationally. It consisted of Amnesty International, Zanzibari students abroad who were supporters of the Umma Party, and the many intellectuals and activists who had got to know Babu in the 1950s and had remained his friends. Most significant among these were veteran political campaigner Fenner Brockway, founder of the Movement for Colonial Freedom, and the organization's general secretary and key organizer, Barbara Haq. Barbara was a remarkable woman who dedicated her life to supporting anti-colonial movements. She set up the Zanzibar Trial Fund, which campaigned tirelessly for the release of Babu and his comrades, and ran a campaign publication – *Habusu* – which was smuggled into Zanzibar.

In a letter to Barbara from prison on December 25, 1976, Babu wrote:

> *Habusu* has become an important instrument of the struggle. It will be extremely useful if you can get it out at least monthly. At the moment it is the only weapon that can secure our liberation. Potentially it can be turned into the famous 'scaffolding' for the 'construction of the building'. Please make sure that as many copies as possible get to Tanzania, especially Zanzibar.[1]

On March 30, 1978, Aboud Jumbe commuted three of the death sentences passed on the defendants, and on April 26, 1978, the 13th anniversary of the Union, Nyerere finally ordered the release of Babu and the twelve other mainland detainees. Although all the mainland detainees were released, the death sentences on four of them – Babu, Ali Mahfoudh, Tahir Ali Salim and Hamed Hilal – were never commuted.

In the midst of the rejoicing at their release, the friends and relatives, many of whom gathered at Babu's house, were acutely aware of the suffering these men had gone through. The sheer scale of injustice,

Release of the Umma comrades on the mainland. Standing first row, left to right: Babu, Martin Ennals from Amnesty International, Ali Mahfoudh, Hashil Seif Hashil; second row, left to right, Suleiman Mohamed (Sisi), Salim Saleh, Haji Othman, Saaban Salim, Tahir Ali; third row, left to right: Amour Dugheish, Martin Hill from Amnesty International, Abdulla Juma, Badru Said, Hamed Hilal; behind the third row is Ahmed Mohamed (Tony). (Photographer unknown.)

the physical and psychological torture, and the daily humiliations had left their imprints. Badru and Tahir Ali died only a few years later. Amnesty had arranged refugee status for Hamed and Hashil, and they left for Denmark eventually. It was only there, Hamed told me, 'after medical examination and care that we regained our confidence'. Ali Mahfoudh left Tanzania to live in Mozambique.

Babu remained in Dar es Salaam for a few months. But with the death sentence still hanging over him, friends and comrades from across the world urged him to leave the country. In 1979, he left Tanzania to take up teaching positions in the United States, first at San Francisco State University and the University of California, and then at Amherst College, Massachusetts in 1981. In 1984 he moved to London and made it his base. He taught at Birkbeck College and contributed to a wide range of publications from *Pacific News Service* to *African Concord, Africa Events, New African,* and *Africa Now.* He was associated with journals such as *Review of African Political Economy* (*ROAPE*), the *Journal of African Marxists* and *Africa World Review*, and institutions like the Africa Research and Information Bureau. While no

Babu with Tajudeen Abdulraheem, general secretary of the Seventh Pan African Congress, and other young activists of the Pan African Movement, March 1994.
(Photographer unknown.)

magazine was too insignificant, or had too small a readership, for him to refuse to contribute an article, many of these seminal writings in the more widely read publications began to reach and inspire progressive activists across Africa and beyond.

In London, vibrant as always, he continued to live his life with an undiminished intensity and optimism, often at the centre of animated discussions, and drawing around him an ever-growing number of friends, comrades, students, supporters and disciples.

In the face of the intensifying economic stranglehold and ideological hegemony of western agencies, Babu wrote of the need for a second liberation of Africa. Always searching for sparks of hope and ready to fan them, he became a close adviser and mentor to a whole range of progressive movements challenging neocolonial military regimes and International Monetary Fund (IMF)/World Bank dominance, such as those at that time in Eritrea, Uganda and Ethiopia.

He was also instrumental in the resurgence of pan-Africanism with a relevance to contemporary conditions. This led to the establishment of a Pan African Movement which held the historic Seventh Pan African Congress in Kampala, Uganda in April 1994, under the slogans 'Resist recolonisation!' and 'Don't agonise, organise!'

At the Congress itself, as Tajudeen Abdulraheem, general secretary of the movement and one of Babu's close comrades during his time in London, was to write, 'At critical stages during heated debates ... he provided intellectual, political and personal leadership that ensured that principles prevailed over opportunism and egos' (Abdulraheem, 1996: 342). However, while he was a steadying influence on the array of different and differing pan-Africanist tendencies at the Congress, his own vision remained that of a united Africa, created not from a union of states but from the united will and solidarity of the revolutionary people of Africa.

Throughout his political life Babu remained a communist, for whom Marxism was not only an ideology but a method of analysis. It was this dialectical approach which enabled him to identify without dogma or sectarianism the forces of progress and change within any situation, while at the same time never losing his commitment to the socialist future of Africa and of the world.

CHAPTER SEVEN

Zanzibar and the Mainland in the Neoliberal Era

More than three decades after the events we looked at in the last few chapters, if we are to believe the media hype, Zanzibar appears recently to have a taken a huge step in the right direction. So what has changed? And what remains the same?

Let us look very briefly at some of the key political changes over the last 36 years. In February 1977, the ASP joined TANU to form the Chama cha Mapinduzi (CCM), and from then on the Isles and the mainland continued under CCM rule. In 1992, a multi-party system was implemented and a new party, the Civic United Front (CUF), was formed. CUF proclaimed itself the voice of the people of the Isles – it did not however represent all the people. Its electoral base, although strong, remained virtually the same as that of the ZNP-ZPPP combination which the British had left in power before the 1964 revolution. Every election since 1992 was accompanied by violence and accusations of rigging.

Babu summarized the situation in the aftermath of the October 1995 election as follows:

> One cannot help noticing the ominous historic parallels with the 1960s, unlike in the mainland, in Zanzibar the balance of political forces has not changed at all .... If in the mainland almost all members of opposition parties left the CCM for ideological or other reasons, in Zanzibar it was different. Here the old party divisions and loyalties ... remained virtually solid as in 1964 .... If CUF is the offspring of ZNP-ZPPP, CCM Zanzibar is ASP in a new garb headed by an amalgam of

progressive and reactionary leadership .... Even political agitations are expressed in the same old language of hostility and rage.

(Babu, 1995: 12)

In 2000, post-election violence escalated further, with the government firing into crowds of protesters, killing 35 and injuring 600. The 2005 elections also saw scenes of serious violence. But the 2010 elections were different: there was no violence and in fact as a result of a series of remarkable political developments, Zanzibar now has a Government of National Unity involving both CCM and CUF leaders. So how was the change achieved? Why did these two parties, whose leaders had been sworn enemies, come together? And what clues do the US and British interventions in Zanzibar in the 1960s provide to help us understand the contemporary political scene? These are the questions we shall briefly explore in the next two chapters, placing them in the context of the reconfigured forces of imperialism today.

By all official accounts the 'reconciliation' between the CCM and CUF has taken hard work. In March 2010, Zanzibar's House of Representatives adopted a resolution that laid out the framework for a Government of National Unity, and for a referendum asking the people of Zanzibar to vote for or against an agreement between the two main parties that whatever the result of the election, the next government would be a coalition. A Committee of Six was then set up to implement the 'reconciliation'.

On July 31, 2010 the referendum took place, drawing 71.9 per cent of the electorate and a 66.4 per cent yes vote. While in earlier elections there had been international observers, this time there was a project, the Election Support Project 2010, funded and supervised by donor and investor countries and agencies including Canada, Denmark, the European Commission, Finland, the Netherlands, Norway, Sweden, Switzerland, the United Kingdom, and the United Nations Development Programme (UNDP). It was managed under the auspices of the UNDP Tanzania.

On October 31 the presidential election was finally held. It produced the coalition government which had been expected. CCM had more votes, so the CCM candidate Dr Ali Mohamed Shein became the president, while the CUF candidate Seif Sharif Hamad became vice president. And then on February 28, 2011 the leaders received a pat on the back from the Americans. The US ambassador

Alfonso Lenhardt conferred the Martin Luther King Drum Major Award on the 'Committee of Six', described in the ambassador's words as the 'bipartisan group of patriots who put aside party politics to do the hard work of implementing reconciliation' (Mjasiri, 2011).

Ali Mzee Ali, the CCM chair of the House of Representatives, who only a year earlier had told US officials privately that CUF was 'not a real party but a breakaway faction of CCM opportunists' (US Embassy, 2009b), made an acceptance speech on behalf of the Committee. He said that the 'leadership of the Zanzibar leaders of both CCM and CUF were able to read the signs in time to avoid the revolutions that were taking place in North Africa'. He also said, adding a touch of farce to the proceedings, that the new government was the 'legacy and vision of the late Abeid Amani Karume [who] had always underscored the importance of equality, reconciliation and unity in Zanzibar'. Zanzibar he said, 'is already an institution and a model of democracy for other countries to emulate!' (Mjasiri, 2011).

In fact, it was not just the Committee of Six who had worked hard to achieve this result. As secret US documents made available by WikiLeaks show, the Americans and their European counterparts, worried about their investments in the region and about the anger of the oppressed and excluded sections of society, had worked hard too, constantly monitoring and shaping events. In this chapter and the next, we look at a few of these documents, and examine what they tell us about the United States's broader concerns today, and the changes and continuities in imperialist strategies in East Africa.

'Development' in Zanzibar and Mainland Tanzania Today

Zanzibar is still a remarkable place but it is no longer the buzzing economically confident centre it was in the 1960s. Industry and agriculture have both declined. The clove industry is all but dead. Tourism has meant that prime coastal land has been taken over by hotels, disrupting people's traditional livelihoods and bringing only very limited benefits to them in return.

A Zanzibar Poverty Reduction Plan set up in 2003 by the UNDP and the UK Department for International Development (DfID), is essentially a platform for donors, its activities consisting mainly of setting up offices for staff, making arrangements to 'monitor poverty' and setting up the infrastructure to manage aid. Poverty is still both acute and widespread. Pemba, which was fairly prosperous before the years of Karume's dictatorship, is now even worse off than Unjuga – starved of resources and with little infrastructure. According to the Zanzibar government's Chief Statistician's Office, 74 per cent of people in the poorest district of Pemba, Micheweni, live below the basic needs poverty line (Ministry of Labour, Youth, Children and Women Development Zanzibar, 2007).

In fact, today, as in the 1990s, Tanzania as a whole is one of the poorest regions of the world, where 42 per cent of children under 5 on the mainland are stunted (TDHS, 2004/05: 218) and for every 100,000 births, 578 women die in childbirth – one of the highest maternal mortality rates in Africa (TDHS, 2009/10).

The country still depends heavily on agriculture, and 50 years after independence colonial cash crops still provide 85 per cent of exports.

In Zanzibar, people often say that the Isles have been excluded from development while the mainland has prospered. But in reality neither the mainland nor the Isles have prospered. Nyerere's Arusha Declaration phase seriously damaged the economy, as we have seen. In the mid-1980s under pressure from the IMF, the World Bank and bilateral donors, the government, now under Nyerere's hand-picked successor Ali Hassan Mwinyi, started the process of economic liberalization. Structural adjustment policies cut into welfare services, and the country was gradually opened up to global capital under the supervision of the IMF. However the government was soon accused of a lack of commitment to 'reforms'. By 1994, relations with aid agencies, financial institutions and the IMF were all badly strained, at least partly because the government's inefficiency made it hard for it to meet their demands.

Mwinyi's successor, Benjamin Mkapa, was also personally chosen by Nyerere who, although retired, remained a controlling figure in Tanzanian politics till his death in 1999. Mkapa was more successful in doing the bidding of international finance. He privatized public corporations with crusading zeal and appropriated, in partnership with his former finance minister, the now defunct but then lucrative Kiwira coal mine (Kaijage, 2012). In addition to privatizations, much of Tanzania was sold off to the robber barons of global capital. The looting of Tanzania's land and resources which has followed ever since is on a colossal scale.

Gold was just one aspect of this loot. Tanzania has the third largest deposits of gold in Africa after South Africa and Ghana, and what happened to those deposits under Mkapa is an example of what neoliberalism meant for the country. In 1975 the first deposits were discovered in the Bulyanhulu area of Tanzania by artisanal miners, and initially the government encouraged them to mine. However, when a Canadian corporate, Sutton Resources, showed an interest, the government sent in the paramilitary to evict these miners, despite a High Court ruling upholding their right to mine. Soon afterwards Sutton Resources sent in bulldozers to close off mine shafts with the approval of the government. This led to an alleged massacre of artisanal miners who were trapped inside the shafts (Lissu, 2002).

In 1999 Barrick Gold Corporation acquired the mines, and this was followed by an investment of US$280 million by international banks, and insurance against political risks to the tune of US$345 million by the World Bank Private Sector Insurance Arm, the Multilateral Investment Guarantee Agency (MIGA) and the Canadian government's Export Development Corporation. In 2000, the Geita mine also commenced production, initially as a joint venture of AngloGold and Ashanti, and later, with the merger of the two companies in 2004, under the ownership of AngloGold Ashanti (AGA). All this was in line with the *Africa Strategy for Mining* technical paper of 1992, developed by the World Bank and the IMF, and the 1998 Mining Act of Tanzania, which was written by investors and monitored by the World Bank (Mgamba, 2012).

So what did Tanzania get out of it all? The fortunes made by Barrick Gold and AGA in Tanzania from 2004 to 2009 provide some clues. In this period US$2.5 billion in gold was exported mainly, through these two companies, but the government has accrued just US$21–22 million per annum on average. In fact, Barrick failed to declare payments in royalties and taxes to the government, its general manager Greg Walker declaring in 2008 that the company will 'only start paying corporation taxes in 2014 when we will begin realizing profits'! (Sharife, 2009). AGA, producing 3 million ounces of gold from the Geita mine, valued at US$1.43 billion at current gold prices, paid taxes averaging US$13 million per annum, which amounts to less than 0.001 per cent of turnover (Sharife, 2009). If the Tanzanian exchequer was, and is, being robbed of billions of US dollars, the sheer exploitation of the surplus value created by the Tanzanian worker, in the mines and the fields is even more startling. If the average return on capital in the developed economies is about 5 per cent (from the exploitation of labour in these countries), in countries like Tanzania in sectors such as gold mining and oil and gas, even in 1982 it ranged from 40 per cent to several hundred per cent (Babu, [1982b] 2002).

Today Tanzania's workforce is being made available to global capital in new ways for some of the worst kinds of exploitation through the establishment of special economic zones (SEZs) and export processing zones (EPZs). In these zones, which often take over prime agricultural land, wages are low, there are few health and safety regulations, trade unionism and all labour laws are banned, and if experiences in other parts of the world are anything to go by, the workers – often predominantly female – face frequent sexual harassment and abuse. US cables (exposed by WikiLeaks) gloat over the fact that in Tanzania, 'greenfield' foreign direct investments (FDI) are allowed through SEZ legislation (US Embassy, 2008b). This means that multinational corporations will be able to enter Tanzania to build new factories and/or stores while receiving subsidies, exemptions from corporate tax payments and other incentives.

In addition, these companies are transferring profits to offshore tax havens almost as a matter of course, leading to a massive loss of revenue for the government. In 2009/10 the transfers were estimated at Sh695 billion, equivalent to the health sector budget in the same period (Mutarubukwa, 2011).

Corruption is rife (and has been for the last two decades), and both foreign capitalists and Tanzanian politicians and businessmen engage in it enthusiastically. It is not however, as is sometimes claimed, inherent to African society. It occurs in the United States and the United Kingdom, and in Tanzania, as elsewhere, it is the financial structures put in place by global capital that create and encourage corruption.

Over the first decade of the 2000s a new scramble for Africa's resources began, and Tanzania handed over land and ocean regions rich in oil and gas, gold, diamonds and other minerals for a pittance, with negligible taxes and a massive repatriation of profits to foreign capital.

As the US Embassy noted approvingly in a cable to the secretary of state and other East African embassies:

> The Tanzanian Investment Center (TIC), established by the Tanzanian Investment Act of 1997, is the focal point for all investors' inquiries and facilitates project start-ups .... Companies holding TIC certificates of

incentive are allowed 100% foreign ownership; VAT and import duty exemptions; and repatriation of 100% of profits, dividends, and capital after tax and other obligations. Similar incentives are offered to investors in Zanzibar through the Zanzibar Investment Promotion Agency.

(US Embassy, 2009c)

According to official estimates, Tanzania has some 44 million hectares of arable land. Nearly one-tenth of this has been requested by investors from the United Kingdom, Germany, Sweden, the Netherlands and the United States to grow jatropha, a source of biofuel. As Dr Felician Kilahama, head of Tanzanian Beekeeping and Forestry, puts it, 'How will jatropha benefit Tanzania? Well, exactly. We have no answers. We want food first, not jatropha' (Mutch, 2010).

Indian companies are acquiring land on leases of 50 years, and in some cases even up to 99 years, at throwaway prices to grow food grains for the Indian and global markets.[1]

Aid and Dependency

With its pro-western stance, Tanzania has long been the darling of multilateral and bilateral donors (despite a brief dip in 'donor confidence' in the mid-1980s). As US chargé d'affaires Michael Owen reported:

> The Scandinavians have their largest development assistance programs in the world here, and the UK, Netherlands, Germany, and Japan also have very large programs. Canada is now set to make Tanzania one of its largest assistance recipients. [However this aid has created] 'donor dependency'.

(US Embassy, 2005b)

Does aid ever create anything other than dependency? As Babu wrote in 1994:

> The need for aid has become a necessary concomitant to our trade relations with developed economies: we trade with them, we lose, we beg them for aid, and more aid. Aid is damaging to both givers and receivers. In most cases especially in the case of voluntary agencies, aid is given in good faith to do good and feel good. The aid donor though, does not realise that his or her high standard of living is maintained at the expense of aid receiving countries whose cheap exports to developed countries are largely based on slave wages .... Take one glaring example,

> Bob Geldof, the British musician, was so moved by the Ethiopian famine of 1984 that he launched a massive charity campaign worldwide that raised $400 million. But generous as no doubt it was, it was only equivalent to two days' transfer of wealth from Africa to Europe and America ... consciously or not aid in effect helps to make this massive robbery acceptable.
>
> (Babu, [1994] 2002)

Maria Baaz has shown that aid not only makes aid givers 'feel good', it enables them to blame the ordinary citizen of the receiving country. That worker or peasant whose labour is being super-exploited to make the developed economies wealthier is described routinely in development discourse as passive and at the same time, and contradictorily, scheming and thieving (Baaz, 2005: 134–47). This approach had been embraced and made his own by Benjamin Mkapa, as Michael Owen noted: 'President Mkapa ... has on several occasions exhorted Tanzanians to "stand on our own two feet," and not to "expect hand-outs forever"' (US Embassy, 2005b).

'The Jewel in the Crown of Tanzania'

Despite the billions made by the mining corporates out of Tanzania's gold, for the West and particularly for United States, today gold is not Tanzania's most precious resource. That is oil. In Libya while 'running up the Stars and Stripes in "liberated" Tripoli ... US Ambassador Gene Cretz blurted out: "We know that oil is the jewel in the crown of Libyan natural resources"' (Pilger, 2011). Tanzania may soon be considered to have a similar jewel in its crown.

Early in 2012, Mustafa Mukulo, the then finance minister (who has since been removed amid rumours of corruption), told the press that with the recent discovery of natural gas in Tanzania, it was all set to become a 'gas economy', with proven gas reserves of 28 trillion cubic feet (tcf) and expectations that this could go as high as 60 tcf. Tanzania has for some time been producing small quantities of gas for domestic consumption from Songo Songo island, but these new mainly offshore finds are on a much larger scale. Currently, almost all major oil and gas corporates – Shell, BP, AGIP, Antrim, Amoco, Texaco, Ophir, British Gas, Tullow, Artumas, Maurel & Prom, Statoil, and Indian companies Reliance and Essar – are operating or negotiating in Tanzania, and the country may receive FDI inflows larger than US$22 billion per year.

British Gas International has already announced an investment plan in excess of US$10 billion in the second half of the decade (Ratio Magazine, 2012).

Among other countries, Norway has had its eyes on Tanzania's and particularly Zanzibar's possible deposits for a while (Chachage, 2009), and Norway's Statoil is currently a major contender in the new scramble for Africa. 'East Africa is hot for us at the moment', declared Tim Dodson, its executive vice president exploration (Williams, 2012).

The Tanzanian government is now setting up the infrastructure for oil extraction as well as the legal framework, a new Petroleum (Exploration and Production) Act and a Natural Gas Master Plan, including design and adoption of a Gas/Petroleum Revenue Management Bill covering taxation and the budget treatment of gas revenues. The exact terms of contracts remain to be seen. Will these contracts mean that oil companies will provide money upfront to Tanzania and then siphon off the bulk of profits? This has been the case in the Democratic Republic of Congo (DRC), for example. Will they be willing to pay for the damage caused by oil spillages? Or will they pay only a comparatively small sum, with liabilities being capped? Platform London, in its study of oil contracts, conflicts, pollution and poverty in DRC, point out that 'Host governments are often distracted by signature bonuses, as they represent hard cash up front. Much of the debate over the contracts has focused on these kinds of payments at the expense of looking at more important provisions' (Platform, 2010: 9).

While these natural gas deposits have been found both onshore in mainland Tanzania and offshore, in Zanzibar petroleum has been discovered, particularly in the so-called Deep Sea Blocks Numbers 9, 10, 11 and 12 which surround Pemba and Unguja. The extent and nature of these deposits are not known, but adequate exploration, let alone exploitation, has been delayed because of a dispute between Zanzibar and mainland Tanzania.

According to a cable sent by US chargé d'affaires Tulinabo Mushingi to the secretary of state and the Departments of Energy and Commerce in Washington:

> Some local representatives for the smaller oil companies, such as Paddy Hoon of Heritage Oil,[2] talk up the possibility of significant finds. Comparing Tanzania's offshore capacity to that of Nigeria, Hoon has

tried to convince all who will listen that the big strike is only one investment away. However, TPDC's [Tanzania Petroleum Development Corporation's] Halfani believes there is no oil to be found near the islands.

(US Embassy, 2009i)

However, Mushingi continued:

> Despite the lack of progress on oil exploration, and the real possibility that exploration will not expose viable fields, the potential for oil is at the center of a political debate between Zanzibar and the mainland. Most Zanzibaris see themselves as an independent nation in free association with the mainland, forming the Union of Tanzania. The issue of gaining exclusive control over any lucrative resources is a hot button for all Zanzibari politicians. During the April 2009 session of Zanzibar's unicameral House of Representatives, delegates from both parties unanimously adopted a resolution tabled by ruling CCM-Zanzibar stating that the laws establishing TPDC and oil exploration activities in the country were not ratified by Zanzibar's Parliament, so under the articles of the Union, TPDC's activities were not recognized in Zanzibar. The resolution reiterated the view that the 1968 agreement on revenue-sharing between Zanzibar and the Union government did not apply to energy and asserted that Zanzibar's share from the mainland was too low. It recommended that Zanzibar form its own TPDC equivalent and that any exploration in Economic Exclusive Zones (EEZ) should be carried out jointly. Any coordination would be handled through the national Vice President's Committee for Union issues, but the resolution stressed that energy, oil and gas as they existed in Zanzibar and its waters were not Union matters. Apparently Shell is unable to explore blocks awarded to it in 2002 because of the standoff.

There are indications that things may change, with Shell being given permission to explore the blocks round Zanzibar.

Regardless of the quality and extent of Zanzibar's oil and how the revenue from it is divided, the finds in Tanzania (and also Uganda and Kenya) have qualitatively altered Zanzibar's position in the context of US imperialism, as we shall see in the next chapter. As part of an East African region rich in oil and gas, which stretches from Mozambique to Somalia, it will be drawn even further into the paranoid US networks which monitor and gather intelligence and regard ordinary citizens as potential terrorists.

People in the rural areas of the mainland where gas has been found, even those who are not Muslims, can sense this. They are not optimistic about the benefits for them of their country's oil and gas. As Thembi Mutch reported, from one village among many others with similar experiences:

> In the small village of Mikindani on the south-eastern coast of Tanzania, World Bank-funded roads sit alongside shattered coral from dynamite fishing and poor sewerage facilities. John, 15, points to the four ships in the distance. 'They're all here because of the oil and gas', he says. 'Sometimes the *wazungu* [foreigners] come in on helicopters. They're not allowed to meet us; there's a ten-mile exclusion zone around their compounds in case they get kidnapped.
>
> (Mutch, 2012)

Village elders in Mikindani are aware that the high unemployment in the region (only 8–10 per cent of the population are employed) is unlikely to be improved since the extraction of oil will not create many jobs for local people.

US Fears of China

While during the cold war in Zanzibar, and later in Tanzania, the US State Department was beset with the fear of 'Chicoms', today Islamic terrorism has replaced communism as a bogeyman for the United States. Despite this, American anxieties about China and China's relations with African countries have not gone away. US discourses on China in Africa today, whether expressed through secret cables to and from the State Department or in journal articles by American academics, reveal an increasing fear of China's growing economic strength and burgeoning trade with African countries.[3]

In the first decade of this century, China increased its trade with Tanzania. The total volume of trade between China and Africa as a whole stood at a massive US$166.3 billion in 2011, compared with US$10 billion in 2000 (Liu Guangyuan, 2012). In exchange for light industrial goods, which many claim are of somewhat low quality, China has been eagerly extracting raw materials, and to facilitate this economic role it has been building and developing infrastructure – bridges, roads and railways. It is providing Tanzania with a $1.2 billion loan to build a 230 km natural gas pipeline linking its gas fields in Mtwara with Dar es Salaam.[4]

In contrast, US strategies in Africa seek to establish a new and total economic and military control of much of the continent. So while Tanzanian papers run stories of US soldiers opening schools and providing humanitarian aid, behind the smiles and promises of help these soldiers are, as WikiLeaks documents show, the propaganda face of a ruthless new army of conquest whose main purpose is to facilitate the plunder of raw materials by US and European multinational companies.

Between 1998–2001 and 2002–05 alone, the United States doubled its military spending in Africa from $296 million to $597 million (Yi-chong, 2006). In 2002 a white paper published by the African Oil Policy Initiative Group (AOPIG) – a Washington lobby group set up by the Israeli think tank, the Institute for Advanced Strategic and Political Studies – recommended 'a new and vigorous focus on US military cooperation in sub-Saharan Africa, to include the design of a sub-unified command structure which could produce significant dividends in the protection of US investments [while] … confronting and eliminating global and regional terrorism' (Glazebrook, 2013; AOPIG, 2002). In December 2006 such a command structure was authorized by the US government. It was called AFRICOM, the United States Africa Command. President Bush announced that it would be based in Africa. However in 2008 this was categorically rejected by the African Union, and in a humiliating about-turn for Bush AFRICOM was housed in Stuttgart, Germany (Glazebrook, 2013).

One of AFRICOM's strategic goals was to confront the increasing Chinese influence on the continent. One AFRICOM study claimed with a touch of cold war hysteria that 'The extrapolation of history predicts that distrust and uncertainty will inevitably lead the People's Liberation Army (PLA) to Africa in staggering numbers' (Holslag, 2009: 23). Whether this happens or not remains to be seen. The US Congress appears to be divided over how to deal with China's activities in Africa, and President Obama's new defence strategy suggests that the Pacific will be the new arena for military tension and possible confrontation (US Department of Defense, 2012). However the US policy of war and plunder in Africa is unlikely to change in the foreseeable future. As John Pilger notes, America is deploying troops in 35 African countries, beginning with Libya, Sudan, Algeria and Niger – a news item which, although 'reported by Associated Press on Christmas Day … was missing from most Anglo-American media' (Pilger, 2013).

US Fears About Iran

Of Dwight Eisenhower's many memorable statements, two are particularly relevant today. The first is a diary entry in 1951 before he became president: 'Lord knows what we would do without Iran's oil'; and the second came two years later at a meeting of the National Security Council on March 4, 1953, where he said that it was a matter of great distress to him that 'we seemed unable to get some of these down-trodden countries to like us instead of hating us' (Robarge, 2008). A few months later the CIA engineered the coup which overthrew the nationalist and highly popular elected prime minister of Iran, Muhammad Mossadeq, who had nationalized Iran's oil, and replaced him with the puppet regime of the repressive Shah Mohammad-Reza Pahlavi.

Today despite a very different government in Iran from Mossadeq's, US anxieties are very similar. US diplomats in embassies in 'down-trodden' countries across the world are busy trying to prevent Iran from establishing friendly relations with those countries, while the CIA is active in Iran, according to Iranian politicians (Dehghan, 2011).

With regard to Tanzania, the United States has had, over the last few years, two main concerns. The first is a fear of Shia 'extremists' influencing the country's Muslims, and the second is uneasiness about Tanzania's stand over Iran's alleged nuclear weapons programme. In their efforts to get Tanzania to toe the US line at the United Nations, we have seen US diplomats cajoling and threatening behind the scenes while Tanzanian politicians respond by capitulating or trying to explain their actions without giving offence.

In January 2006, for example, the US Embassy in Dar es Salaam cabled Washington that Ambassador Liberata Mulamula, head of the Multilateral Division of Tanzania's Ministry of Foreign Affairs, believed:

> that discussion on referring the Iran situation to the U.N. Security Council (UNSC) needs to wait until the IAEA [International Atomic Energy Agency] has met and made a formal recommendation. Since Iran is a signatory to the Non-Proliferation Treaty (NPT) .... Preemptive actions not within the NPT parameters could possibly provoke Iran to withdraw from the NPT, as occurred with the Democratic Peoples Republic of Korea in 2003.
>
> (US Embassy, 2006a)

It further reported that Mulamula had said, clearly because she was not entirely happy about the domineering US approach, that 'the GOT [Government of Tanzania], currently chair of the UNSC, be kept apprised of developments in the USG [US Government] approach, including the next steps we intend to take. "No surprises; please let us know what you are planning to do."'

Another cable to Washington a couple of years later, in December 2007, revealed deputy chief of mission (DCM) Purnell Delly chiding Tanzania's deputy foreign minister Seif Ali Iddi that 'if nuclear issues had not been an issue during the recent trip [of Vice President Shein] to Tehran, then they should have been', and asking for a public statement 'urging Iran to cease its enrichment program and fully cooperate with the IAEA'. Iddi replied that Tanzania had in fact insisted to the government of Iran that 'they should come clean' and also that Tanzania had been in debt-relief discussions with the government of Iran (US Embassy, 2007b). Tanzania still has unpaid bilateral debts to Iran, which has yet to provide debt relief (Munte, 2012).

The secret cables from US diplomats in Dar es Salaam on the subject of Iran underline their faith in Tanzania's current president, Jakaya Kikwete. For example, in January 2009 chargé d'affaires Larry André recorded his dismay about defence minister Hussein Ali Mwinyi's visit to Tehran and the signing of a memorandum of understanding (MOU) regarding sharing of military and defence expertise. But he also noted also that according to home minister Lawrence Masha, not only did the MOU not 'represent a shift in Tanzania's relationship with Iran or the acquisition of military weapons or equipment', such a policy shift 'would have required approval by an interagency body chaired by President Kikwete' (US Embassy, 2009j). Jakaya Kikwete, as we shall see, is the United States's man, perhaps more willing to do their bidding than any of his predecessors.

CHAPTER EIGHT

US Interventions in Zanzibar and on the Mainland Today

As far back as 2003, when Benjamin Mkapa was the president, the Tanzanian government was already deeply involved in the war on terror and carrying out abduction and 'extraordinary rendition' under US orders. One case which has come to light and is currently before the African Commission on Human and Peoples' Rights is that of Al-Asad, a Yemeni citizen who had been living and working in Tanzania since 1985. He was arrested at his home in Dar es Salaam in December 2003, bundled into a waiting plane and flown to Djibouti, where he had never been before. There he was detained in a secret prison, and according to Interights, an international centre for the legal protection of human rights, he was interrogated by a US agent and tortured. He was eventually taken to an airport where he encountered a 'rendition team' – a gang of black-clad individuals who stripped and assaulted him before chaining and hooding him and forcing him to board another plane. He was held in secret CIA prisons in Afghanistan and Eastern Europe and finally taken to Yemen in 2005. He was released in 2006, never having been charged with a terrorism-related offence. According to Solomon Sacco, an Interights lawyer working on the case:

> This case is the first filed before the African Commission on rendition in Africa, but it is far from an isolated case, evidence continues to emerge of a systematic global practice of rendition. This case is part of a growing demand for recognition and justice for victims of rendition that will not go away. States—like Djibouti—who cooperated with the United States in its rendition programs, violating their own laws as well

as the African Charter in the process, must be held accountable by the African Commission.

(Interights, 2011)

Another case which also illustrates Tanzania's involvement in extraordinary rendition is that of Laid Saidi, an Algerian citizen. It is one of several cases highlighted in a report by the Open Society Foundation (2013). Saidi, an Algerian citizen, was apprehended in May 2003 by Tanzanian police, and after three days in prison in Dar es Salaam, was driven to the Malawi border and handed over to uniformed Malawian authorities. He faced what amounted to psychological torture and humiliations before being transported to Afghanistan in horrific conditions. In Afghanistan he was held in three CIA prisons including the infamous 'Dark Prison' and 'Salt Pit'. About a year later, he was flown to Tunisia where he was detained for another 75 days before being returned to Algeria, where he was released.

Since Kikwete came to power in December 2005, Tanzania has become an even more eager participant in the 'war on terror'. He clarified his stand in a meeting with US ambassador Retzer in May 2006:

> Tanzanian President Kikwete made clear he wishes not only to continue existing cooperation on counterterrorism, but to expand it. He pointed specifically to training and technical assistance from the FBI, U.S. Civil Aviation authorities, the Treasury Department, Justice Department, and other agencies, and said he wants to expand such programs. In the run-up to President Kikwete's May 17–18 visit, we urge Washington to develop proposals to build on President Kikwete's interest.
>
> (US Embassy, 2006c)

In Kikwete's time in office, East Africa's role in the global networks of the US 'war on terror', as revealed by the Al-Asad case, has increased and intensified, and the infrastructure for counterterrorism (CT) work funded mainly by East African countries themselves has become more organized. Yemen's National CT Centre is held up as a model by the United States in this respect.[1]

US ambassador Mark Green wrote, for example, in an 'Update on Tanzania terrorist issues' in February 2008:

> The establishment of a Tanzanian National Counterterrorism Center is a priority for Tanzania .... However, plans and a timeline for the center are progressing slowly due to limited funding. To enhance the GOT's

[Government of Tanzania's] understanding of the benefits of National CT Center, in October 2007 S/CT [the Office for the Coordinator for Counterterrorism: US State Department, 2001–09] funded the trip for one officer from the TISS [Tanzania Intelligence and Security Service] counterterrorism unit and one officer from the CT unit of the National Police to visit Yemen's National CT Center in Sana'a. Both officers recognized through this experience the necessity to finalize and fully staff Tanzania's National Counterterrorism Center, but budget constraints remain.

(US Embassy, 2008c)

By June 2009, the United States was happier with Tanzania's commitment to the 'war on terror'. As Ambassador Retzer reported, in a 'Scenesetter for Deputy Secretary Lew visit to Tanzania':

[While the first US strategic priority in Tanzania is] building the GOT's counterterrorism (CT) capacity and promoting security .... The Government of Tanzania (GOT) has embarked on a serious effort to establish its own CT Center. On December 4, the [US State Department's] Anti-Terrorism Assistance (ATA) Program launched a three week workshop in Dar es Salaam to facilitate a comprehensive discussion with Tanzanian authorities on how to set-up and equip such a unit. There was full engagement from the GOT, with participants ranging from the police and military, to immigration and intelligence, to customs and banking. According to ATA trainers, who have hosted similar workshops in Senegal, Kenya, and Chad, Tanzanian officials have clearly 'taken ownership' and have demonstrated that they are ready and willing to embark on this endeavor.

(US Embassy, 2009a)

Increasingly, human rights abuses against Muslims in East Africa are being justified in the name of fighting terrorism, with US officials claiming that the individuals involved are linked to the bombings of the US embassies in Dar es Salaam and Nairobi in 1998.[2] At the same time there are an increasing number of references to the 'Swahili coast' and the links between the populations from Zanzibar via Mombasa to Somalia. These links are at best tenuous, but Somalia's experience does have some lessons for the Isles, particularly in the context of Zanzibar's possible oil deposits. In Somalia too, in the early 1990s, it was oil that the United States was seeking – nearly two-thirds of Somalia's reserves had been allocated to the US petroleum giants Conoco, Amoco, Chevron and Phillips in the period before Somalia's pro-US president, Mohamed Siad Barre, was overthrown. It was these investments, not human beings, that the United States was trying to protect when in the name of 'humanitarian intervention' it invaded Somalia in December 1992. As Babu predicted then, the US invasion was simply seeking 'to establish a precedent in international law to enable the US to intervene in any Third World country in the future with impunity ... couched in the rhetoric of humanitarianism and human rights' (Babu, [1993] 2002).

The invasion of Somalia, almost exactly a year after the fall of the Soviet Union, was one of the markers of a new period when, with the cold war over, the United States which was suddenly bereft of an enemy would create and target a new one – Islamic terrorism. In line with this came discourses like that established by Samuel Huntington, who divided the world into eight cultures – 'Western, Confucian, Japanese, Islamic, Hindu, Slav-Orthodox, Latin American and perhaps African' ('perhaps' because he was not sure whether Africans had a culture) – and claimed that it was culture, not politics or economics, that would divide the world. This was because 'only the West valued "individualism, liberalism, constitutionalism, human rights, equality, liberty, the rule of law, democracy, free markets". Therefore the West (in reality the United States) must be prepared to deal militarily with threats from these rival civilizations' (Ali, 2002: 299).[3]

Today oil companies are once again exploring the rich oil deposits of the Dharoor valley and the Nugaal valley, for example, while troops from the United States, the United Kingdom, Ethiopia and other 'peacekeepers' stand at the ready. Off the coast of Somalia, as Suzanne Dershowitz and James Paul wrote:

> a powerful naval flotilla has [since 2008] patrolled the seas .... More than thirty nations have sent warships – including aircraft carriers, frigates, destroyers and other heavily-armed vessels – as well as many sophisticated military aircraft. Officially, the naval forces are protecting the sea lanes from pirates – Somalis in small boats who have seized merchant ships and their crews for ransom. The United Nations Security Council has repeatedly endorsed the naval operations, warning of the pirates' threat to safe passage for the world's maritime fleets and their 'threat against international peace and security in the region'.
> (Dershowitz and Paul, 2012: 1)[4]

The US Military's Role in Tanzania

Tanzania is of course very different from Somalia. It is well known for its 'stability'. Why then are there so many US soldiers around in the country? What is their role, and who gives them permission to arrive and depart? The secret documents exposed by WikiLeaks provide us with some interesting clues.

A 'Scenesetter' produced by the US Embassy in June 2009 for the visit of deputy secretary of state Jacob Lew to Tanzania, for example, noted that:

> In December 2006, the GOT gave approval to ... [the] Combined Joint Task Force–Horn of Africa to establish a Civil Affairs presence on the Swahili Coast. The Civil Affairs team (which we have rebranded as 'AFRICOM') is carrying out humanitarian projects and helping build Civil Military Operations (CMOs) ... capacity within the Tanzania Peoples Defense Forces (TPDF).
>
> (US Embassy, 2009a)

If jargon makes this message somewhat opaque, a clarification is available from the US Joint Chiefs of Staff website. CMOs (like the ones whose capacity is being increased within the Tanzanian military) are activities, it tells us, where the military takes on a host of civilian roles in order to facilitate military operations, to consolidate and achieve US objectives. They can take place in a friendly, neutral or even hostile operational area, and involve the military working to 'establish, maintain, influence, or exploit relationships' with governments, NGOs, local authorities, and ordinary civilians, and even in some instances perform 'the activities and functions of local, regional and national government. These activities may occur prior to, during, or subsequent to other military actions' (US Joint Chiefs of Staff, 2008). The aim of the CMOs being established within the Tanzanian military therefore is to use the Tanzanian armed forces, government and NGOs to facilitate military activities which further the interests of the United States, and to take over the activity and function of the Tanzanian government, as and when needed by the US state.

As the definition of CMOs continues, 'at the strategic, operational and tactical levels and across the full range of military operations, civil military operations CMOs are a primary military instrument to synchronize military and nonmilitary instruments of national power'. The 'potential challenges' that CMOs would also deal with are highly significant. Not only do they include 'ethnic and religious conflict, cultural and socioeconomic differences, terrorism and insurgencies, the proliferation of weapons of mass destruction', but 'sharpening competition/exploitation of *dwindling natural resources*' (italics added).

In other words, just as 'collateral damage' is an euphemism for the deaths of civilians, CMOs are an euphemism for a variety of unsavoury and illegal activities. They cover actions such as surveillance, abduction, rendition, torture, providing bases for drone aircraft and support for military actions to secure the resources that the United States wants from Africa. In the context of East Africa, 'dwindling natural resources' clearly include oil and gas. To 'achieve operational US objectives' to gain control of oil is therefore not only justified but a duty for the US army.

In fact, acquiring oil has come to be regarded in military-academic discourse as a sort of modern equivalent of the colonial 'white man's burden'. It is the duty of US forces, in other words, to deal with Africans, however unpleasant a task they may think this is, and make their countries 'stable' in order to acquire the dwindling resource of oil. There is no mistaking the overt racism in these lines from a paper written by an ex-commander of the US Coast Guard who is now at the US Joint Forces Staff College's quaintly titled Joint Advanced Warfighting School:

> Many, perhaps most, of the big oil producers in Africa – Nigeria, Angola, Cameroon, Gabon, and Equatorial Guinea – are cesspools of corruption, poverty, and collective misery. Yet, in order to ensure a stable energy supply, world markets need these countries to be reasonably stable.
> (Coleman, 2009: 19)

The East African Community and the War on Terror

The list of countries provided by Coleman is of course not up to date, since over the last few years it has become clear that some countries in East Africa – Uganda, Kenya and also Tanzania – have large deposits of oil and gas. With an awareness of this, the US military has established frameworks and strategies for intervention not only in individual countries but in the region as a whole – and what is more convenient than to use the 'war on terror' to justify and strengthen these interventions?

The East African Community (EAC) which came into being in 2000 provides an entry point for US control. It is, on the face of it, the latest in a series of attempts at regional cooperation, all of which were unsuccessful. In earlier incarnations, the Community included only Uganda, Kenya and Tanzania. Now it has two new members, Rwanda and Burundi. As before, the Kenyan government appears to be dominant. However, it does not seem to matter because the other two main members, the Tanzanian and Ugandan governments, are just as eager to facilitate US and European aims as the Kenyan government is. The EAC has clearly moved a long way from the pan-Africanist goals which its earlier incarnations had espoused. Its role in the war on terror and its facilitating of AFRICOM's work have increased rapidly.

For example, in February 2008, US ambassador Mark Green's report, 'Update on Tanzania terrorist issues', revealed the early stages of the US use of the EAC in the war on terror:

> There is limited GOT cooperation with regional partners on CT issues through the East African Community (EAC), which now includes Kenya, Uganda, Burundi and Rwanda in addition to Tanzania. These five nations cooperate through an EAC program: the East African Regional Strategy for Peace and Security .... In late 2007 the GOT established a relationship with the Government of Sudan; however, the extent of CT cooperation is unknown. The GOT also has worked bilaterally with the Kenyan government on CT issues in the past and Tanzania has a permanent position in the Interpol Office in Nairobi. In addition, the National Police have good contacts with many of their regional neighbors, and have participated in regional CT programs with officers from neighboring countries through programs at the USG-funded International Law Enforcement Academy (ILEA) in Gaborone, Botswana.
>
> (US Embassy, 2008c)

By early 2010, the US relationship with the regional organization was more established. Let us look at US communications during just three days in the life of the EAC – February 2, 3 and 4, 2010 – and see what they reveal about senior East African politicians and their remarkably subservient relationship with the United States. In the first cable, descriptively titled 'East African legislature could be vehicle for U.S. regional goals' (US Embassy, 2010a), Ambassador Lenhardt reported on his meeting with Abdirahim Abdi of Kenya, who was the speaker of the East African Legislative Assembly (EALA), an organ of the EAC:

> Abdi said that ... bills passed by the EALA had the force of law among

all members. Abdi said trans-border issues like trafficking or money laundering, and perhaps anti-terrorism and human rights guarantees, were areas where the EALA could play a key role.

The next day, Lenhardt reported on a meeting with the EAC secretary-general, Juma V. Mwapachu – a Tanzanian politician who was appointed ambassador extraordinary by Kikwete and nominated to this post. Lenhardt informed Washington that Mwapachu had told him that the EAC states were working on an MOU on joint military cooperation and would welcome inputs from AFRICOM, and that 'while the five East Africa Community states are at peace at this time, the history of the Great Lakes region (including EAC members Burundi and Rwanda) has largely been one of instability'. Mwapachu had appealed to Lenhardt for help to reinforce the military relationship between the EAC and AFRICOM, which he described as 'a force for stability in the region'. Lenhardt also said that 'once an MOU was signed, then the EAC could work to establish a mil–mil relationship with AFRICOM more directly .... Mwapachu would like to see more cooperation in terms of counterinsurgency, peace-building and peace keeping, with operations on both land and sea' (US Embassy, 2010b).

On February 4, Lenhardt was once again a bearer of good news for the United States, this time about the Tanzanian People's Defense Force (TPDF) which, since the appointment of a new chief of defense forces, General Davis Mwamunyange, in 2007, had been 'upgrading the TPDF's aging military hardware', had become more involved in regional matters and international peacekeeping operations, and had grown closer to the US military. The credit according to Lenhardt had to go to Kikwete, because:

> while General Mwamunyange has presided over these changes, it would be a mistake to attribute the changes to him alone. The philosophical shift started two years prior when Jakaya Kikwete became the President of Tanzania ... within ten days of General Mwamunyange's assumption of command, U.S.–Tanzanian military relations shifted noticeably .... Over the next 18 months senior leader engagement visits by U.S. military leaders from Africa Command (AFRICOM), Naval Forces Africa (NAVAF), U.S. Army Africa, Marine Forces Africa (MARFORAF), and in particular the Combined Joint Task Force–Horn Of Africa (CJTF-HOA) served to further strengthen the bilateral relationship.
>
> (US Embassy, 2010c)

Building 'Sources' and 'Resources'

In the cold war period, an essential part of US covert activities was the use of lethal 'direct actions'. These methods have, of course, been developed further for use in the war on terror, particularly under Obama. As *The Nation* reported in June 2010, elite special forces teams working for the Joint Special Operations Command had been deployed under the Obama administration in 'Iran, Georgia, Ukraine, Bolivia, Paraguay, Ecuador, Peru, Yemen, Pakistan and the Philippines .... The frontline for these forces at the moment, sources say, are Yemen and Somalia' (Scahill, 2010).

According to the *Washington Post* (quoted by Scahill):

> The Special Operations capabilities requested by the White House go beyond unilateral strikes and include the training of local counterterrorism forces and joint operations with them. Plans exist for preemptive or retaliatory strikes in numerous places around the world, meant to be put into action when a plot has been identified, or after an attack linked to a specific group.

These military activities, like those of the cold war, require networks of informers and other similar forms of surveillance on the ground. Charles R. Stith, US ambassador to Tanzania from 1998 to 2001, emphasized the importance of such networks and sources:

> [O]ur ability to capture the terrorists in the Dar bombing was significantly enhanced by the coordination and cooperation of the Tanzanian and South African intelligence services. Africa's fight against terrorism can only be enhanced by such efforts. Correspondingly, there needs to be more intelligence gathering and sharing in cooperation with international entities and bilateral partners.
>
> (Stith, 2010: 64)

Linked to such intelligence services is the monitoring of Muslim populations for signs of anti-Americanism. This is something that has gathered pace after 9/11, when as Mahmood Mamdani wrote:

> after an unguarded reference to pursuing a 'crusade', President Bush moved to distinguish between 'good Muslims' and 'bad Muslims'. From this point of view 'bad Muslims' were clearly responsible for terrorism [while] ... 'good Muslims' were anxious to clear their names and consciences of this horrible crime and would undoubtedly support 'us'

in a war against 'them'. But this could not hide the central message of this discourse: unless proved to be 'good', every Muslim was presumed to be 'bad'.

(Mamdani, 2004: 15)

Increasingly, the United States and the United Kingdom have launched well-funded programmes to try to create such pro-western 'good Muslims'. The Citizen Dialogue Program was one such project. As Karen Hughes, US undersecretary for public affairs, put it in 2006, the program was:

> a strategic imperative ... to isolate and marginalize the violent extremists, confront their ideology of tyranny and hate. We must undermine their efforts to portray the West as in conflict with Islam by empowering mainstream voices and demonstrating respect for Muslim cultures and contributions. That's why I've spent so much time reaching out to Muslim Americans.
>
> (Hughes, 2006)

As WikiLeaks cables show, however, such reaching out was not always welcome. In one instance, visiting American Muslims who were part of the Citizen Dialogue Program 'were surprisingly refused entry to a mosque in downtown Dar es Salaam'. As they tried to enter the mosque a crowd gathered and blocked their way, protesting because they were Americans. Later the visitors were told by 'moderate Muslim leaders' in Dar es Salaam that 'radical youth', possibly Iranian-backed radical Muslims, were responsible for the incident (US Embassy, 2007c).

Despite this, US diplomats think they have been successful in this respect in the Isles. In June 2009, the 'Scenesetter for Jacob Lew' stressed the importance of winning the 'hearts and minds' of the people: 'Our work in Pemba – a majority Muslim island – exemplifies this strategy', it said. 'We have knit together cultural preservation projects to repair historic mosques, self-help projects to improve rural livelihoods, and significant USAID malaria control and education programs' (US Embassy, 2009a).

'Militant Youth' and the Government of National Unity

In Zanzibar as elsewhere, the rise of anti-Muslim racism globally, the attacks by the West on countries with majority Muslim populations, and the atrocities committed on Muslims in these countries and others in the name of fighting terrorism have all served to strengthen the sense of Muslim identity. Here in addition there is the constant portrayal, particularly for tourist consumption, of the slave trade as intrinsically Islamic or Arab.

It is this strong Muslim identity itself, particularly among young people (making them in US terminology 'militant Islamic youth'), that the United States fears today. As for the combination of 'militant Islamic youth', unemployment and discontent, this has for a number of years been regarded as automatically equating to 'extremism' and possibly even 'terrorism', and this in turn has shaped a variety of US diplomatic and foreign policy imperatives.

For example, Michael Retzer, the Republican politician and US ambassador to Tanzania, was clearly disconcerted about the following news with which he cabled Washington on August 24, 2006:

> three hundred young supporters from the Civic United Front (CUF) surrounded their party leader, Maalim Seif Hamad, demanding answers .... Venting their frustrations and demanding a response from Hamad, these angry youth drew attention to both the stalled reconciliation process on Zanzibar as well as the leadership void within CUF .... What is the CUF leadership's plan? And where is President Kikwete on his promise for reconciliation?
>
> (US Embassy, 2006b)

Retzer continued that he had investigated further by holding confidential meetings with 'respectable observers of the Zanzibar political scene', to explore these issues. Dr Rwekaza Mukandala, director of the NGO Research and Education for Democracy in Tanzania (REDET), was one such person. Retzer reported his views 'that CUF youth are losing patience and looking for leadership', although Hamad was still popular, especially in Pemba. 'Some Pembans are so loyal to Hamad that they claim to see his face on the moon!'

Despite a reassurance from Dr Mukandala that there was little chance of the disaffected youth splintering off from CUF, Retzer remained concerned, as he noted in his report, that 'this very inaction and lack of political strategy, combined with the outburst of angry youth, bears careful watching'. REDET suggested to the ambassador that the answer was 'youth education and leadership training as a long-term approach to creating future leaders'. Mukandala told him that this was something with which the United States could help, by equipping 'the next generation of Zanzibari leaders with effective negotiation and conflict management skills'. Clearly REDET was happy to be involved in supplying a pro-US 'next generation of Zanzibari leaders'. Retzer reported that he intended to create a group international visitor programme in the next year for young CUF and CCM leaders.

As WikiLeaks revealed, the United States is eager for a Tanzanian government of national unity which includes CUF. This is not only because it would shore up the present leaders, weakening the possibility of youth militancy and creating 'stability'. Such a government would also have the advantage of making it possible for Americans to do business with CUF leaders and supporters. According to another informant, Dr Ndumbaro from the University of Dar es Salaam and a colleague of Dr Mukandala at REDET, the CUF members were easier to work with since 'CCM has yet to create an enabling environment for the private sector to flourish ... many businessmen and traders are key CUF supporters'.

Things moved slowly in this context, however, and a year later, an increasingly impatient Retzer was still pushing the CCM towards reconciliation. Tanzanian foreign minister Bernard Membe assured him that the CCM, led by President Kikwete, was 'working day and night' to resolve this issue, although 'at least two major hurdles still lie ahead: the CCM Central Committee and President Karume's willingness to implement whatever reconciliation agreement may be reached' (US Embassy, 2007a).[5]

On July 18, 2008, the US Embassy in Dar es Salaam summed up its policy in a document entitled 'Zanzibar primer: the issue, why it matters and what we are doing about it' (2008a). In language strikingly similar to that in secret documents of the 1960s which were concerned about the spread of communist influences from Zanzibar to the rest of Africa, the primer voiced US anxieties about Zanzibari political Islam which could spread to other parts of the continent:

> Counterterrorism: Zanzibaris are among the al-Queda members involved in the 1998 attack on this mission. There are pockets of extremist support throughout the Swahili cultural region (the coasts of Kenya and Tanzania, Zanzibar and the Swahilophone Comoros islands). *The reservoir of unemployed, desperate, hopeless, angry and alienated Islamic youth for terrorists to recruit from is greater in Zanzibar*

than elsewhere in the Swahili cultural area. Family and commercial links within the Swahili world are such that repercussions of events in one place are felt elsewhere in the region. Increased radicalization in Zanzibar would infect the whole region. Conversely, a settlement that led to improved governance and increased prosperity would decrease the attraction of extremist ideology throughout the region

(US Embassy, 2008a, my italics)

Whereas in the 1960s, 'regional stability' (which really means a safe climate for Western capital) was to be achieved by subsuming Zanzibar into Tanzania, and strengthening Nyerere's position, in recent years it seems to have been about strengthening Kikwete and about establishing a CUF-CCM government in Zanzibar to snuff out the militancy of Zanzibari youth, identified as potential Islamic terrorists:

> Regional Stability: President Kikwete is nearly three years into what is likely to be a ten year stay in office. Tanzania is having some success at reforming itself and is a net contributor to regional stability. *It is important to U.S. interests that Kikwete's presidency is successful and that he continues to adhere to an agenda of economic and governance reforms.* He has publicly committed to Zanzibar reconciliation as a top goal of his administration. Failure to achieve that goal will hurt the president's political standing and will allow Zanzibar to continue to blemish Tanzania's international image.
>
> (US Embassy, 2008a, my italics)

To fulfil these and other aims, the US mission was to encourage Zanzibaris and the Union government to achieve a political settlement. And, the document notes, the United States was in a position to do so since its 'extensive interagency assistance programs in Zanzibar ... give us great standing with the Zanzibari people and with political leaders from both camps, allowing us to speak out on Zanzibari political issues as a proven friend of the islands' people'.

Diplomats and Donors Try to Play 'Hard Ball'

The road to the Government of National Unity was however full of pitfalls and frustrations for the United States. By January 2009 the US Embassy was noting that Kikwete seemed to have changed his approach. In his speech at a rally in Zanzibar his 'boasts about Karume's leadership in delivering Zanzibar development were disingenuous ... for the opposition, who might have been listening for an opening toward reconciliation, calling them "drunkards" was not helpful' (US Embassy, 2009d).

To check out the CUF's reaction, US officials spoke to a man they were close to. The CUF's foreign affairs advisor, Ismail Jusa, was a 'U.S. International Visitor Program alumnus'. Jusa told the Embassy staff that Kikwete had recently changed his tune, using language which echoed 'the battle cry of those revolutionaries who carried out violent punitive actions on Pemba'; that he and Seif Hamad were the 'only real moderates' left in the CUF, and their credibility after successive failures was 'on its last shreds'; and that Juma Duni, the CUF deputy secretary-general, 'was non-compromising and one who would have CUF take a more radical approach'. Jusa also emphasized that there needed to be an international commission of some sort that would guarantee a CUF victory after a free and fair election. 'After attaining power', Jusa said, 'CUF would "clean house"' (US Embassy, 2009e).

While in earlier phases diplomats might share their anxieties and discuss their strategies with top journalists like Colin Legum, for example, today their concerns appear to be discussed routinely with donors. Wikileaks provides us with a glimpse of the exasperation, the anxiety and also the innate paternalism of the high-powered and broad-based European and American group of diplomats and donors who were involved in pushing for fair elections as the first step to a Government of National Unity on these small islands.[6]

One such meeting, for example (discussed in US Embassy, 2009f, under the heading 'Zanzibar: donors seek common position on elections, political reconciliation'), was attended by a host of ambassadors and chargés d'affaires from the United Kingdom, Norway, Finland, France, Germany, the Netherlands, Canada, Japan, Belgium, Ireland, Italy, Spain, Switzerland and the European Commission; the UN country director; representatives from UNDP and the UK DfID; political counsellors from Denmark, Norway, Sweden, the United Kingdom and Canada; and the United States's own Zanzibar affairs officer. (We might well wonder why Zanzibar was so important for all these representatives of the west.) On this occasion, as US chargé d'affaires Mushingi reported:

> The soon-to-depart Dutch Ambassador Van Kesteren called on delegations to play 'hardball.' Donors should draft a common letter to ZEC

(Zanzibar Electoral Commission) with agreed-upon minimum conditions that needed to be present on the ground by a specific date, say November or December 2009. Should those conditions not be met, then donors would 'pull the plug' on paying for or otherwise supporting the elections, labeling them a fraud .... Sweden concluded that 'Kikwete holds the key' toward any broad-based change of tone in the islands.

(US Embassy, 2009f)

A few weeks later, an incident occurred in Pemba which highlighted Norway's concerns over voter registration. WikiLeaks cables reveal how this led to the diplomats trying to 'play hardball' with Zanzibar's CCM, with disastrous diplomatic consequences. On that day a number of CUF supporters going home after a successful and peaceful boycott against voter registration organized by the party were attacked by Special Forces police, who fired into the air before chasing them, arresting two people and beating one man severely. Panicking that this could lead to youth violence, disrupt the election and end their hopes of a Government of National Unity, a 'Friends of 2010' group of diplomats and donors issued a statement, calling for the observance of international standards and democratic processes for the entire 2010 election process, with a specific focus on Zanzibar. However, as the US Embassy informed Washington, Karume responded with an out and out snub:

> The diplomats were called and told that Karume took exception to references in the joint statement that implied there was any Union Government role in the registration and ID processes underway in Zanzibar .... Karume suggested the Joint Statement was a product of ignorance on the part of the Friends.
>
> (US Embassy, 2009g)

The 'Friends' retreated. As the US Embassy told Washington, they decided to keep pressing the Union Government and President Kikwete to maintain peace and order in Zanzibar, and CUF to avoid anti-democratic actions and violence. And they also agreed that they had to navigate carefully to avoid giving the appearance of working on CUF's behalf (and especially to avoid giving CUF that impression), since 'CUF's reliance on international attention makes the threat of condemnation of its own tactics a powerful lever for us' (US Embassy, 2009h).

Over the next two years, the process of pushing CCM and also

CUF continued until after many ups and downs, the elections were held peacefully in 2010, with an acceptable degree of transparency. They led finally to a Government of National Unity. What this government will deliver largely remains to be seen, but one thing is certain: given the events that have followed, the United States may not be happy with the degree of 'stability' achieved.

Zanzibar and the Future

Kikwete is ready to reassure the United States that he is totally under its command, and that Tanzania (both the mainland and Zanzibar) under his leadership will place US interests above all else. In the Isles, however, things are a little less clear in this respect, because there is an increasingly palpable discontent about the Zanzibar's relationship with the mainland.

In September 2009, I was able to interview Juma Duni, then deputy secretary-general of CUF, whom his colleague Ismail Jusa had described to US diplomats as 'non-compromising' and 'radical'. The highly articulate Duni (who is now minister of health in the Government of National Unity and rather less vocal about the Union) identified domination by the mainland as one of his party's key concerns:

> At the beginning, after the Union, we had only 11 Articles of the Union; now there are 23. As time goes on the government of Zanzibar gets weaker and weaker. For example, if a minister of the Republic of Tanzania goes to the US and talks about agriculture, they listen. If a minister from Zanzibar talks about agriculture they say 'Who are you? The Minister was here a few days ago and aid and loans were agreed with him.' That aid and those loans do not come here [to Zanzibar], they go to the mainland. So they use the United Republic for the benefit of Tanganyika. Donors deal with them as the United Republic. Zanzibar becomes like a municipality. We go there and ask their consent instead of being a part of the union.

Duni was also concerned about financial issues:

> Before the Revolution there was an East African Currency Board. Zanzibar was a member with Tanganyika, Uganda, and Kenya. We met as four countries. Using constitutional and legal methods they removed Zanzibar and took all our assets. They used that money to establish the Bank of Tanzania. We would have thought that the Bank of Tanzania

is for all of Tanzania and we would get equal treatment when we go for grants or loans or short-term finance. But we are not allowed to go to that Bank, we have to go to the Minister of Finance. He has to agree to it and then he tells the Bank. So the Bank does not belong to us .... For the last forty years we have been arguing that we are shareholders, we have a right because of the assets you took from us.... Also they have added foreign exchange – which was not originally a Union matter.

(interview with Juma Duni, 2009)

The demands for greater autonomy for Zanzibar have for years been widespread on the Isles, where many are bitter about mainland domination. But gradually public debate has intensified. Some of the donors and governments who pushed for the Government of National Unity have indicated that they too are not averse to greater autonomy for Zanzibar. For example, in a paper titled 'Concept note providing strategic transitional support for the Zanzibar Government of National Unity', the International Law and Policy Institute (ILPI), a legal NGO close to the Norwegian government, pointed out that Zanzibar's economy is largely controlled by the Union and for 47 years the Union has done very little to stimulate growth and eradicate human hardship in the Isles (cited in Rashid, 2011: 15). The ILPI states, somewhat ambiguously, that Zanzibar can develop on its own. The underlying message seems to be that greater autonomy is the answer.

At the same time CUF and some Zanzibar CCM leaders have been pressing for oil and gas to come under Zanzibar's control, and in October 2012 a tentative agreement was finally reached, possibly also under pressure also from oil and gas corporates. In October 2012 Zanzibar started the process of establishing the legal and institutional arrangements to manage its oil and gas reserves (Bariyo, 2012).

If the agreement is ratified and economically viable deposits of oil found, how will it affect Zanzibar's future? Will the government be able to avoid the pitfalls common in contracts with oil companies, such as their refusal to pay anything but a tiny share of the profits and a pittance as liability in the case of accidents? Such accidents have, after all, been commonplace in Africa, causing enormous environmental damage and displacement. For example Tullow Oil, which is already active in Tanzania, had considerable spillages in Ghana in 2009 and 2010 (Platform, 2012); ChevronTexaco spilled oil from its offshore platforms in northwest Angola in June 2002, polluting beaches and forcing fishermen to stop work (BBC News, 2002); and Statoil, which is like to be a major player on the mainland as well as in Zanzibar, recently spilled huge amounts of oil in the Russian tundra (Staalesen, 2012). Shell, which is currently exploring in the seas around Zanzibar, is notorious for its spillages and the environmental destruction of the Ogoni people's lands in the Niger delta. Evidence revealed in 2010 also implicated Shell in 'financial and logistical involvement with the Nigerian military and [Nigerian] Lt-Col Okuntimo' who murdered four Ogoni elders, an incident which led to the execution of Ogoni people's leader Ken Saro-Wiwa (Rowell and Lubbers, 2010).

There is also the question of who within Zanzibar will benefit. In almost every oil-rich country in Africa, a stratum of corrupt super-rich intermediaries have emerged from among the political elite and have colluded with the corporations to crush and silence dissent. So far, despite the enormous scale of inequalities in the country, the need for a more equitable distribution of resources among Zanzibar's people does not seem to be on the agenda for either CUF or CCM.

With the promise of oil and gas hanging in the air like a mirage, the future of the Union has become a subject of acrimonious debate within the Government of National Unity. And it is against this background that the Tanzanian government has finally launched an attempt to consult the public about the type of Union they would like to see. The consultation is to be followed by a Constitutional Review in the 2013 parliamentary session. The chair of the Constitutional Review Commission, Judge Joseph Warioba, has repeatedly said that Tanzanians should be free to air their views on the Union (Mugarula, 2012). However, in a display of democracy Zanzibar style, the second vice president Seif Ali Iddi, a member of CCM, has announced categorically that 'This Union is here to stay', and the prime minister Mizengo Pinda, also CCM, has declared that 'the union shall not break' (Dodma, 2012).

Not only is Zanzibar CCM's official position on the Union unchanged, inflexible and diametrically opposite to that of CUF, the party will also not brook dissent from its own members. Mansoor Yussuf Himid, a CCM member and minister for agriculture and tourism, who said on July 14, 2012 that the two-government arrangement in the Union between Zanzibar and Tanganyika was 'outdated' and he would not 'accept the issue of natural gas and oil remaining on the list of union matters', had his appointment as a member of the Revolutionary Council 'nullified' by President Shein (Yussuf, 2012).

With the leadership of CUF and CCM conducting an angry debate amongst themselves in the Government of National Unity, the demand that Zanzibar should become a sovereign state has been voiced most forcefully by an organization which is registered as an NGO – the Association for Islamic Mobilization and Propagation (AIMP), known as *Uamsho* or awakening in Kiswahili. AIMP attracted American attention back in 2005 (US Embassy, 2005a), with Michael Owen, US deputy chief of mission and chargé d'affaires in Dar es Salaam, describing it as 'among the most vocal of Zanzibar's small fundamentalist organizations ... consisting of a few dozen relatively young clerics with a Saudi Wahabist orientation ... the CCM party views Uamsho as a stalking horse for the opposition CUF party'. Owen went on to describe how:

> Just over a year ago, when a series of small explosions rocked Zanzibar's Stonetown, several Zanzibari government officials publicly linked Uamsho and the CUF party, and blamed both for the attacks. Dozens of activists from both the NGO and the political party were arrested, but all were eventually released without charge .... The government's accusations against Uamsho are part of a longstanding pattern, in which the CCM attempts to portray CUF as the party of Islamic extremism and violence .... Uamsho itself might have provided the Zanzibari government with a convenient fundamentalist target.
>
> (US Embassy, 2005a)

By 2012, the AIMP was no longer small. Its public rallies drew thousands and it was taking an openly political stand, campaigning against the Union and blaming it for fleecing Zanzibar economically. Unemployed young people who see no future and are angry at the visible inequalities are drawn to the group in large numbers. The government has responded with increasing repression.

At the end of May 2012 a large church on the outskirts of Stone Town was stormed by an angry mob and badly burned. This was immediately blamed on the group despite strong denials of any involvement by AIMP leaders. Less than two months later, in the wake of the sinking of a Dar es Salaam to Zanzibar ferry which claimed an estimated 145 lives and was blamed on the government's failure to enforce safety regulations, there was another major incident. Mourners, some of whom were supporters of the AIMP, had gathered outside a mosque to offer prayers for the dead when they were set upon by the police, sprayed with tear gas, beaten up and arrested (Reuters, 2012).

In the last week of October 2012, Sheikh Farid Hadi, a spiritual leader of the AIMP, went missing for three days. The anger of his supporters spilled out onto the streets. Tear gas, street battles and arrests of more than a hundred people followed. The police denied any knowledge of his whereabouts, but when Hadi resurfaced, he said he had been blindfolded, taken to an unknown location and interrogated about the AIMP's future plans and his own frequent trips to Oman and other Arab countries (Zakaria, 2012). Meanwhile, the AIMP is already being described in the media, without a shred of evidence, as linked to Somalia or even Boko Haram, the Islamist group which is involved in large-scale sectarian violence in Nigeria (Jorgic, 2012).

So what, in fact, are the AIMP's broader politics? What does it say about oil, big business, unity in the Isles and redistribution of resources? In an email interview in July 2012, a spokesperson told me that he thought the Government of National Unity was a positive step because it 'facilitated cooperation between Zanzibaris'. Of the two main political parties, CUF had become 'too silent after joining the government' and CCM was a party in decline 'because they are not representing the people of Zanzibar'. On the subject of oil, AIMP would like all dealings 'to be transparent and handled by Zanzibaris'. As for the future development of Zanzibar, the organization regarded Brunei as a 'role model', because, the spokesperson told me, Brunei is 'a very peaceful country [where] they use [oil and gas] for the development of their citizens'.

What has led to this vision for the future? Zanzibar after all has few similarities with Brunei, which is a conservative Islamic monarchy where the Malay elite live off the labour of non-citizens. Perhaps these aspirations reflect a lack of information. Perhaps there is a distant echo too of the old right-wing ZNP ideology which regarded ASP members and supporters as outsiders and not 'Zanzibar's people'. Either way, AIMP's energy is undeniable, and so is its support from a significant proportion of the population across the 'Arab–African' divide and also across class divisions.

As this book goes to press, the government has once again lashed out against the AIMP. Sheikh Farid Hadi and other leaders of the organization have been arrested and are in prison, where they have been humiliated and denied basic religious rights – being forced to have their beards shorn and being denied the opportunity to offer their obligatory prayers, for example. Meanwhile, a new six-member committee has been set up to take this debate further. By and large its members support the widening campaign for a sovereign Zanzibar linked through a treaty to a sovereign Tanganyika (Machira, 2012). Among its members are many the United States would approve of: Ismail Jusa, a former US International Visitor Program alumnus; Eddy Riami, a prominent businessman; Hassan Nassor Moyo (CCM), whose role in the 1960s and 1970s I have discussed in earlier pages; and ex-minister Yusuf Himid.

Not on the committee but closely associated with it is Salim Rashid, who was once an Umma member but changed his approach drastically and went on to help design, among other things, the liberalization and reform package adopted by Zanzibar in 1984. Rashid's views for the future are outlined in a paper which has become a kind of neoliberal manifesto for this committee and other politicians pressing for an autonomous Zanzibar (Rashid, 2011). In it he recommended 'robust and affordable credit facilities for the private sector with low interest rates' and foreign experts to develop Zanzibar into a free zone based mainly on banking, business process outsourcing, insurance, information and communications technology, tourism, and other financial services 'It is imperative', he wrote, 'that all development schemes and projects are carried out with the extensive consultation and active participation of globally respected and qualified international experts ... with traceable and extensive track records advising Government' (Rashid 2011: 3). In other words he advocated for consultants from the IMF, World Bank and western governments who are advising pro-US regimes across Africa, and who Rashid would like to see in charge of exploiting Zanzibar's land and people. Rashid recommended that Zanzibar should seek the collaboration of Norway and Qatar insofar as its oil and gas are concerned. Having expressed his gratitude to all major donors, he ended by singling out the role of the United States: the 'United States particularly being a leading donor to Zanzibar can play a strategic role with the cooperation of other donors in transforming our economy and the way of life of our people' (Rashid, 2011: 18).

What kind of autonomy will Zanzibar attain if it is so subservient to the United States, which after all was once covertly responsible for the Union? A shiny neoliberal Zanzibar, sovereign or not, will bring enormous wealth to a few politicians and intermediaries, but make life harder for everyone else, and particularly for those who live in the poorer areas of the Isles. The 'disaffected angry youth' identified by US diplomats, whose numbers have risen, and many of whom now support the AIMP, will not be stakeholders.

What would Babu have thought of these debates? In 1994, he wrote about the nature of the Union and possibilities for change. He too argued for a sovereign Zanzibar linked by a treaty to the mainland because, he wrote, the present relationship 'has enabled the latter to act ... as a protector of one of the most reactionary and backward-looking regimes ... which obstructed the educational and economic development of the people' (Babu, 1994: 32). He pointed out that the Union had denied Zanzibar the right to negotiate and enter into economic arrangements which were of exclusive advantage to it, but not necessarily to the mainland, and brought the Isles 'under the leadership of a political party whose vision is limited only to security concerns and a distorted, almost myopic view of economic development' (Babu, 1994: 32).

Control of Zanzibar's currency from the centre, he argued, had denied Zanzibar the right to have an independent monetary and financial policy suitable for its own development strategy. 'The reckless resort to the printing press to finance the mainland's perennial deficits always drags Zanzibaris into inflations not of their own making which makes it very difficult to embark on any economic and social planning .... Zanzibar should have the right to self determination to work for and secure the best interests of the people of Zanzibar' (Babu, 1994: 32).

How did Babu visualize the economic development that would secure these interests? In 1996, when he died, Zanzibar's oil deposits were not considered economically viable, so he never wrote about their contribution to the development of the Isles. However his approach to development meant that he would not have liked to see control of these deposits handed over in totality to multinational companies. He would have pointed out perhaps that blueprints for independent national exploitation of gas do exist, not only in Venezuela but in Bolivia and Argentina. These countries have used oil and gas for some remarkable economic and political developments. In Bolivia, for example, in the four years between 2004 and 2009 illiteracy was eliminated, the infant

Qullatein Badawi, Hashil Seif Hashil and Khamis Ameir in Zanzibar on June 28, 2011
Source: Mailys Chauvin.

mortality rate was reduced from 52.1 to 43.4 per 1,000 live births, and a state pension was created. Land and power were redistributed for the first time in 500 years. Much of this was paid for by royalties from oil and gas (Taylor, 2009; Tradingeconomics, 2013).

Babu's vision for Zanzibar, which he wrote about and discussed in various magazine articles (see for example Babu, 1994), focused on its people, its land and its strategic position. Always a realist, he could see that Zanzibar would have to regenerate its economy after the destruction wrought by the post-Union years, and transform its economic priorities to realign them towards its people's needs. He argued for a planned and internally integrated economy which would involve the development of the only two economic sectors which create new wealth – agriculture and industry. Everything else – insurance, commerce, tourism and so on – 'depends on the ever expanding wealth created from these two vital sectors. If either of them is in trouble the whole economy is in trouble, because this is the real economy.' To revive this real economy, he wrote, it was urgent, first to rebuild the infrastructure (Zanzibar had and still has no modern water supply system, sewage system, or regular electricity supply, for example), and it was toward this that the majority of external loans must go. Second, agriculture, particularly food production, but also non-food crops must be modernized, not by bringing in multinational corporates as is happening in mainland Tanzania, but by giving local producers help and incentives.

Third, the construction industry and the building of public and private housing must be prioritized. It would not only provide affordable homes but open up cement and lime production, lumber and carpentry industries, manufacture of wiring, roofing and other components of a modern construction industry, and also branch out into construction of roads, railways, irrigation canals and so on. It would create several thousand new jobs annually – increasing people's spending power and developing the home market. Production would then be to satisfy the needs of Zanzibar's people, not primarily for export.

The government, he wrote, must take the initiative to encourage local entrepreneurs whose current investment in commerce could be diverted more profitably to manufacturing industry, supplemented if need be with some foreign technical and financial inputs.

In the context of this approach it is clear that this is where future revenues from oil might be used for investment – in domestic production and to develop the home market, and also eventually manufacture industrial goods that could be exported competitively to the rest of East Central and Southern Africa, and to the Gulf and Red Sea area in the north.

Babu's vision, arguably, is that of a Zanzibar that might have been. But it is also a possible Zanzibar of the future. With the failure of neoliberalism and the suffering and murderous exploitation of capitalism in decline, ideas like Babu's are now more important than ever before. They are being studied once again by those who want liberation from imperialism and economic justice. Perhaps in the future they will inform the development of a different socialist Zanzibar. And if on the face of it Zanzibar has changed, as the documents I have referred to in this book show, today, behind the everyday interactions of politicians, and often supervising them as in the cold war years, are the military and economic representatives of imperialism – ready to intervene directly if all else fails. Babu's reflections, written 40 years ago at the end of his introduction to Walter Rodney's *How Europe Underdeveloped Africa*, are if anything even more relevant today:

> If by looking into the past we have known the present, to know the future we must look into the past and the present. Our action must be related to our concrete experience, and we must not give way to metaphysical hopes and wishes – hoping and wishing that the monster who has been after us throughout our history will someday change into a lamb. He won't.
>
> (Babu, [1971] 2002)

APPENDIX ONE

A People's Programme: The Political Programme and Constitution of the Umma Party

The Umma Party of Zanzibar is a people's party, organized as a conscious vanguard of the oppressed people of Zanzibar. It represents the broad interests of the African people who today are bearing the brunt of economic oppression resulting from foreign colonialism and local feudalism. While today it fights relentlessly against imperialist oppression, its ultimate aim is socialism: that is, the abolition of a system of exploitation of man by man.

'A People's Programme' of the Umma Party is a clarion call to action, a consistent, constructive action to ensure a quick replacement of an obnoxious system which has so far degraded the people of Zanzibar, bodily and mentally, to subhuman condition. This obnoxious system must be replaced by a socialist system which alone can ensure the true dignity of man.

Membership to the Umma Party implies sacrifice. To a member of the Umma Party no task is insurmountable. Spinelessness has no place among our ranks and personal suffering can never deter us from pursuit of our ultimate objective, namely socialism. The Umma Party cannot tolerate the existence of opportunists, self-seekers among its ranks, and will be vigilant against the infiltration of such destructive elements. The Umma Party is a serious Party of the people and its members are expected to serve the people selflessly and without any desire for reward or personal gain.

Criticism and self-criticism must be conducted fearlessly in accordance with the discipline of the Party. Undisciplined criticism, therefore, cannot be tolerated. Mistakes must the criticized in the manner of correcting them and not for the purpose of exhibitionism. The Party must oppose self-conceit.

Members of the Umma Party, being servants of the people, must wholeheartedly be at the service of the people. They must be permanently in contact with the broad masses of people, understand their needs and help them in solving their own problems.

Every party member must work tirelessly to strengthen the unity and solidarity of the Party. Only in a strong unity can we really serve the people and bring about the social change that will be truly to the benefit of the people. The Party requires each of its members to work actively to bring about the realization of this Programme and all decisions of the Party in order to abolish once and for all capitalism, feudalism, imperialism and neo-colonialism from the face of our motherland.

Constitution of the Umma Party of Zanzibar

NAME: The Party shall be known as the UMMA PARTY

Aims and Objects (National)

(1) Independence now and the development of Zanzibar on the basis of socialism.
(2) To serve the dynamic vanguard for removing all forms of oppression, exploitation of man by man and for the establishment of a socialist society.
(3) To secure unity of all the people of Zanzibar and unity of people of East Africa and the whole of Africa on the basis of Pan-Africanism.
(4) To work with and in the interests of the Trade Union Movement and workers' organizations in joint political and other action consistent with the constitution and political Programme of the Party.
(5) To promote the political, social, economic and cultural emancipation of the people, especially those who depend directly upon their own exertions by hand or by brain for the means of life.
(6) To establish a socialist state in which all men and women shall be equal and have equal opportunity and where there will be no capitalist exploitation.

International

(1) To work with other nationalist, democratic and socialist movements in Africa and other continents with a view to abolishing imperialism, colonialism, racialism, tribalism and all forms of national and racial oppression and economic inequality among nations, races and people, and to support all actions for world peace.
(2) To support the demands of the people for an East African Federation and for Pan-Africanism by promoting unity of action among the peoples of Africa

Membership

(3) Any person may become a member of the party who accepts the Programme and Constitution of the Party, belongs to and works in one

of the Party's organizations, observes the Party's decisions and pays Party membership dues.
(4) The duties of the Party member shall be as follows:
   (a) To endeavour to raise the level of his consciousness and to understand the fundamentals of socialism and the theory of African revolution.
   (b) To observe Party discipline strictly, to participate actively in inner-Party political life and the struggle of the people of Zanzibar, to carry out in practice the policy and decisions of the Party and to fight against everything inside and outside the Party which is detrimental to the Party's interests.
   (c) To serve the masses of the people, to consolidate the Party's connection with them, to learn their needs and to report them in good time, to explain the policy of the Party to them.
   (d) To set an example in observing the discipline of the Party and our organizations, to master his own line of work and to set an example in the various fields of constructive work.
(5) The rights of the Party member shall be as follows:
   (a) To participate in free and fair discussions in Party meetings and Party publications, of the problems concerning the carrying out of Party policy.
   (b) To elect and to be elected within the Party.
   (c) To submit proposals or statements to any Party organizations, up to and including the Central Committee.
   (d) To criticize any Party functionary in Party meetings.
(6) A person maybe admitted as a Party member only after attaining the age of 18.

Application for individual membership shall be made in a duly prescribed form which shall be filled in by the applicant and passed to a Branch Secretary for consideration by his committee as to acceptance or otherwise. On enrolment every member will be supplied with enrolment and dues cards.

Admission Fee: Each individual member of the Party shall be requested to pay an enrolment fee of two shillings upon joining.

Monthly dues: Each individual member of the Party shall pay a monthly due of fifty cents to the Party through a local branch.

Membership (Affiliated)

Affiliate members shall consist of the following:
(a) Trade Unions including Civil Service Organisations;
(b) Peasant and Agricultural Organisations;
(c) Co-operative Societies, Unions and Associations;
(d) Organizations of professionals, artisans and technicians;
(e) Youth, students and sports organizations;
(f) Women's organizations.

i) All such organizations must accept the objects, policy and programme of the Party.
ii) They must in the opinion of the Central Committee be bona fide organizations.
iii) An organization wishing to affiliate shall forward a resolution to that effect, duly signed by its President and Secretary.
iv) Each organization upon being accepted for affiliation must pay an affiliation fee of 25 shillings.

Organizational Structure of the Party

(1) The Party's organizational structure shall be based upon democratic centralization, centralism on the basis of democracy under centralized leadership. The fundamental principles are as follows:
   (a) The leading bodies of the Party at all levels must be elected;
   (b) The leading bodies of the Party at all levels must submit reports at fixed intervals to the lower Party organizations which elect them;
   (c) Each individual Party member shall obey the Party organization to which he belongs; a minority shall obey the majority; the lower Party organizations shall obey the higher Party organizations and all constituent Party organizations shall obey the Central Committee;
   (d) Party discipline shall be strictly observed and Party decisions carried out unconditionally.
(2) Party organizations shall be established on the basis of geographical divisions.
(3) The organizational structure of the Party shall be as follows:
   (a) For Zanzibar as a whole, there shall be the National Party Congress, the Central Committee and the National Party Conference;
   (b) For Unguja and Pemba separately they shall each have an Island Party Congress, Island Party Committee, and Island Party Conference;
   (c) For constituencies there shall be a Constituency Party Congress, Constituency Party Committee and Constituency Party Conference;
   (d) For factory, enterprise, street, office, school there will be a general membership meeting, the Branch Party Committee and the Branch Party Conference.
(4) The highest leading body of a Party branch shall be the general membership meeting of the branch. The highest leading body of a city, constituency or island shall be its Party Congress. The highest leading body of the whole Party shall be its National Party Congress.

During the intervals between Party Congresses at all levels, the Party Committees elected there from shall be the highest leading bodies of the Party organizations of the corresponding levels.

(5) The leading bodies of the Party at all levels shall be established by the elective method whenever possible. They will be elected by a Party Conference or appointed by a higher Party organization only when

circumstances do not permit the calling of a general membership meeting or a Party Congress.

(6) The election of a Party Committee at any level shall be conducted either by a secret ballot or by open vote from a list of candidates, with the guarantee that the voters shall have the right to criticize any candidate and change any candidate on the list.

(7) In order to transmit or to discuss important decisions of a higher Party organization, or in order to review or plan its work, a Party organization at any level may hold various kinds of meetings of its cadres or of its active elements.

(8) Before decisions are reached, every Party member may carry on within the Party and in Party meetings free and full discussions to express his views on Party policy and on various issues. However when a decision is reached, it must be abided by and carried out unconditionally.

(9) In order to promote the creative power of the Party membership, to strengthen discipline which should be conscious not mechanical discipline, to ensure correct Party leadership and to maintain and consolidate centralism based on democracy, the leading bodies of the Party organizations at all levels shall carry out their work in accordance with the principles of inner party democracy.

(10) Party organizations at all levels shall ensure that newspapers under their guidance popularize the decisions and policies of higher Party organizations and of the central Party organ.

(11) On questions of national character, before the Central Committee has made any statement or decision, departmental or lower Party organizations or their responsible personnel should not make any statement or decision at will, although they may hold private discussions or make suggestions to the Central Committee.

(12) The establishment of a new Party organization shall be approved by a higher Party organization to which it belongs.

(13) In order to carry out various kinds of practical work, a Party Committee at any level may, under its leadership, set up departments or commissions to take charge of Party affairs and mass work, as the situation may require. A Party committee at any level, may establish temporary commissions or departments to carry out special, temporary kinds of work.

The Central Organization of the Party

(1) National Party Congress

The National Party Congress shall be decided upon and convened by the Central Committee. Under ordinary conditions, it shall be convened annually. Under extraordinary conditions, it may either be postponed or convened earlier as the Central Committee may decide.

If lower Party organizations representing more than one half of the total membership request that a National Party Congress be convened, the Central Committee will act accordingly.

A National Party Congress shall be recognized as valid only if it is attended by delegates representing over one half of the total membership.

The number of delegates to National Party Congress and the procedure governing their election shall be determined by the Central Committee.

The functions and powers of the National Party Congress shall be as follows:

(a) To hear and receive, discuss, and ratify, the reports submitted by the Central Committee and other organs;
(b) To decide upon and amend the Party programme and Party constitution;
(c) To determine the basic orientation and policy of the Party;
(d) To elect the Central Committee.

(2) Central Committee

The number of members of the Central Committee shall be determined by the National Party Congress.

When vacancies occur in the Central Committee they shall be filled by the interim members of the Central Committee according to the order of precedence.

The Central Committee shall represent the Party in its relations with other political parties and organizations, set up Party organs and direct their activities, and take charge of the distribution of the Party's personnel and funds.

The Central Committee shall be summoned to meet in plenary session once in every month by the Central Political Bureau. However the Central Political Bureau may postpone or call the session earlier according to circumstances. Interim members of the Central Committee may attend the plenary session and have the right to state their opinions.

(3) The Central Political Bureau

The Central Committee shall elect in plenary session the Central Political Bureau, the Central Secretariat and the Chairman of the Central Committee.

The Central Political Bureau shall be the central leading body of the Party and direct all the work of the Party during the interval between the plenary sessions of the Central Committee.

The Central Secretariat: The Central Secretariat shall attend to the daily work of the Central Committee according to the decisions of the Central Political Bureau.

The Chairman: The Chairman of the Central Committee shall be concurrently the Chairman of the Central Political Bureau and the Central Secretariat.

The Central Committee shall according to the needs of its work set up departments (such as Organization Department, Propaganda Department, etc.) commissions (such as Party Press Commission, etc.) and other organs to function in their respect fields to function under the direction and supervision of the Central Political Bureau, the Central Secretariat and the Chairman of the Central Committee.

(4) National Party Conferences

During the interval between National Party Congresses the Central Committee may convene a number of National Party Conferences, composed of representatives from lower Party Committees to discuss and decide upon questions related to Party policy in the current situation.

The representatives to the National Party Conference shall be elected at the plenary sessions of the Island Party Committees and other Party Committees directly under the Central Committee.

National Party Conferences must be attended by representatives from more than one half of the total number of Island Party Committees.

National Party Conferences shall have the power to remove full or interim members of the Central Committee who are incapable of discharging their duties, and to elect in by-elections, part of the interim members of the Central Committee provided that the number of interim members so elected shall not at any one conference exceed one-fifth of the total number of both full and interim members of the Central Committee.

Decisions at National Party Conferences and the removal or election of full or interim members of the Central Committee by the conference shall take effect only on ratification by the Central Committee.

All decisions of National Party Conferences, ratified by the Central Committee, must be carried out by all organizations of the Party.

The Island Organisations of the Party

An Island Party Congress and an Island Party Committee shall accept the leadership of the Central Committee or its representative body.

(1) Island Party Congress

The Party Congress of Unguja or Pemba shall be convened annually by the Island Party Committee. Under extraordinary conditions, the Island Party Committee may either postpone or convene the Congress earlier. An Island Party Committee must convene such a Congress at the request of more than half of its subordinate Party organizations or its representative body.

The number of delegates to an Island Party Congress, and the method of their election, shall be determined by the Island Party Committee, subject to the approval of the Central Committee or its representative body.

The Island Party Congress shall hear and receive, discuss and ratify the reports submitted by the Island Party Committee and other Party organ of the island concerned, and elect the members of the Island Party Committee and delegates to the National Party Congress.

(2) Island Party Committee

The Unguja or Pemba Island Party Committee shall elect in plenary session its Standing Committee, and its Secretary and Assistant Secretary to carry out its daily work. The Secretary of the Island Committee shall be approved by the Central Committee. The Island Party Committee shall meet in plenary session at least once every six months.

The Island Party Committee shall carry out within its Island the decisions of the Island Party Congress and of Central organs, set up various Party organizations, allocate Party personnel and funds and direct the work of the Party fractions in non-Party organizations.

(3) Island Party Conferences

During the intervals of Island Party Congresses, an Island Party Committee may convene a number of Island Party Conferences composed of representatives from constituency Party Committees and other Party Committees directly under it, to decide and discuss on problems concerning the work within the Island concerned.

The Island Party Conference shall have the power to remove, and elect, in by-elections, part of the members of the Island Committee, provided that the number of the members removed or new members thus elected, does not exceed one-fourth of the total members of the said Committee. The decisions taken at an Island Party Conference, and the removal or election of members of an Island Committee by the said conference, shall take effect only upon ratification by the Island Committee.

The Constituency and City Organizations of the Party

The regulations governing the organization of, and work of, the Party for a constituency or city shall be the same as those governing the organization and work of the Party for an Island as set above. Each shall be under the leadership of a superior Party organization.

The Basic Organizations of the Party

The basic organization of the Party shall be the Party Branch. The Party shall establish Branches in all towns and villages. A branch shall consist of at least 25 members. Each branch shall be governed by a Branch Party Committee which shall be elected annually at a general meeting of the Branch.

A Party branch shall strive to bring about a close unity between the Party and the masses of the people. The duties of a Party Branch shall be the following:

(a) To carry on propaganda and organizational work among the masses in order to gain acceptance of the standpoint advocated by the Party and the decisions of the higher Party organizations;

(b) To pay constant attention to the sentiments and demands of the masses, to support such sentiments and demands to the higher Party organizations, to pay heed to the political economic and cultural life of the people, and to organize the masses to solve their own problems;

(c) To recruit new members, to collect Party dues, to check and verify the records of the Party members;

(d) To educate the Party members and organize their studies.

Discipline

Party organizations at all levels may take the following disciplinary measures, according to the actual circumstances against failure to carry out the decisions of a higher Party body or the decisions of the Central Committee or against violation of the Party constitution or Party discipline:

(a) Disciplinary measures applicable to an entire Party organization shall be: reprimand, partial reorganization of its leading body, dismissal of its leading body, and appointment of an interim leading body, or dissolution of the entire Party organization and re-registration of its membership.

(b) Disciplinary measures applicable to a Party member shall be: private admonition or warning, public admonition or warning, removal from assigned work, placing on probation, or expulsion from the Party.

When a full or interim member of the Central Committee of the Party commits a serious breach of Party discipline, the Central Committee shall have the power to remove him from the Committee or even to expel him from the Party. Such measures must be approved by two-thirds of the entire membership of the Central Committee before coming into effect.

The Party member or Party organization against whom a disciplinary measure is taken shall be notified of the reason. Any such member or organization who regards the disciplinary measure as unjust, may challenge the decision and request a reconsideration of the case, or may appeal to the superior Party organization. Party committees at the appropriate levels shall forward such appeals without delay. Delaying or suppression of such appeals is forbidden. Expulsion from the Party is the most severe of all inner-Party disciplinary measures. All Party organizations shall exercise the utmost caution in making such a decision, or approving it, and shall carefully listen to the Party member concerned and examine the circumstances of his mistakes.

The Party's positive object in commending or taking disciplinary measures against a Party member shall be the education of the Party membership and the masses of the people as well as the Party member concerned and not the encouragement of personal vanity or penalization. The criticism and disciplinary measures against Party members who have committed errors are intended to help them overcome their errors and also to serve as a warning to others.

Party Funds

The Party shall be financed by Party membership dues, by income from productive and other economic enterprises operated by the Party, and by contributions from non-Party circles.

APPENDIX TWO

Charge Sheet: Case no. 292 of 1973 (the Umma Defendants)

Accused

State Full name, Address, Sex, Age, Nationality and Tribe.
1. Ahmed Badawi Qullatein, Mwarabu, Mtanzania. Miaka 42, Muislamu, Shirika la Kilimo na Ardht. Wa Vuga, Zanzibar.
2. Ali Mshangama Issa Mngazija, Mtanzania, Miaka 32, Muislamu, M.V. Afrika, Afisa wa tatu, wa Zizi la Ng'ombe Zanzibar.
3. Amar Sailm (Kuku), Mshihiri, Mtanzania, Miaka 42, Muislamu, Idara ya Siha (Usafirishaji) wa Mbuyuni, Zanzibar.
4. Miraji Mpatani, Mtanzania, Miaka 42, Muislamu. Karani mambo msiige wa mpirani, Zanzibar.
5. Abdulla Ali Khamis (Mapara) El-Harusy, Mtanzania, Miaka 36, Muislamu Jeshini, Kapteni. Makao Makuu ya Jeshi unguja.
6. Hassan Makame Seif, Mtanzania, Miaka 26, wa Makadara/Kariakoo/ Bavui Camp, Unguja.
7. Ishaka Haji Juma Harakati, Mtumbatu, Mtanzania, Miaka 25, Muislamu, Dereva wa Mheshimiwa Khamis Abdulla Ameir wa Baraste Kipande, Unguja.
8. Mohamed Abdulla Ahmed, Baramia, Mtanzania, Miaka 41, Muislamu, Mwangalizi wa Ghala, Idara ya Elimu wa Kikwajuni, Unguja.
9. Mohamed Said Mtendeni, Mtanzania, Miaka 37, Muislamu, Mwandishi wa Habari wa China, wa Vuga, Unguja.
10. Rashid Mohamed Ahmed Fallahy, Mtanzania, Miaka 30, Muislamu, Shirika la Mafuta na nguvu za Umeme, wa Vikokotoni, Unguja.
11. Mussa Shabani Khatibu, Mwafrika, Mtanzania, Miaka 30, Muislamu, Makao Makuu wa Wizara ya Fedha wa Vikokotoni, Unguja.
12. Said Saulm Said (Baesi), Mtanzania, Miaka 37, Muislamu, Fundi, Shirika la Umeme wa (Mafriji) Kiponda, Unguja.
13. Saleh Ali Saleh, Mngazija, Mtanzania, Miaka 45, Muislamu, Fundi Shirika la Umeme wa (Mafriji) Kiponda, Unguja.

14. Nurbhai Issa Nurbhai, Mtanzania, Miaka 34, Muislamu, Hana kazi, wa Vuga, Unguja.
15. Kadiria Mnyeji Abdulla, Mwafrika, Mtanzania, Miaka 32, Muislamu, wa Kikwa Mwanasheria idara ya Kilimo, wa Kikwajini, Unjuga.
16. Haroub Mohamed Sailm Mauly, Mtanzania, Miaka 28, Muislamu, Storekeeper, State Fuel & Power, Pembe, wa Vuga, Unjuga.
17. Saidi Mohamed Said (Tumbo) Mwafrika, Mtanzania, Miaka 31, Muislamu Karani Idara ya Flimu, wa Kikwajuni, Unguja.
18. Mohamed Abdulla Seleman (Saghir), Arab. Mtanzania, Miaka 33, Muislamu, Fundi wa Mitambo, Idara ya Habari na Utangazagi, Zanzibar, wa Vuga, Unjuga.
19. Yusuf Ramadan Yusuf (Mhiyao) Mtanzania, Miaka 28, Musilamu, Askari wa Polisi wa Kidongo Chekundu, Unguja.
20. Abbas Mohamed Ahmed, Mngaziga, Mtanzania, Miaka 34, Muislamu, Post office wa Kisiwandui, Unguja.
21. Mohamed Salim Suleiman, Mzaramo – Mtanzania, Miaka 36, Msaidizi wa fundi Mitambo, Idara ya Habari na Utangazaji, wa Raha Leo, Unguja.
22. Mohamed Ali Ladha, Ismaili, Mtanzania, Miaka 30, Muislamu, Bookshop Mapinduzi wa Mwembetanga, Zanzibar.
23. Abdulla Mussa Mohamed (El-Mauly), Mtanzania, Miaka 31, Muislamu Mkuu wa Mashine, Kiwanda cha Sigara, wa Forodhani, Unguja.
24. Mohamed Abdulla Seif (Panya) Labir, Arab, Mtanzania, Miaka 23 Muislamu, Mpishi Kwa Nassor Ali, wa Shangani, Zanzibar.
25. Ali Hemed Houmoud, Mwarabu, Mtanzania, Miaka 23, Muislamu, Kiwanda cha Kusagia Nafaka, wa Kipinda, Unguja.
26. Rashid Mohamed Rashid, Mtanzania, Miaka 23, Muislamu, Kiwanda cha Kusagia Nafaka, wa Kipinda, Unguja.
27. Seif Said Hamad. Arab, Mtanzania, Miaka 34, Muislamu, Mchunguzi wa hali ya hewa, Airport, wa Kiembe Samaki, Zanzibar.
28. Hussein Mbarouk Kombo, Mwafrika, Mtanzania, Miaka 47, Muislamu, Karani wa Majenzi Mapya, Michenzani, wa Sokomoko, Unguja.
29. Ibrahim Omar Soud (Mbisa), Mtanzania, Miaka 31, Muislamu, Depot Manager wa Wesha Caltex, Chake chake, wa Chachani, Chake Chake Pemba.
30. Khamis Abeid Omar, Mtanzania, Miaka 32 Depot Manager wa Caltex, Chake chake, wa Chachani, Chake Chake Pemba.
31. Mohamed Khelef Mohamed, Miaka 32, Muislamu, Depot Manager wa Caltex, Chake chake, wa Chachani, Chake Chake Pemba.
32. Mohamed Ali Seif Ismail, Mtanzania, Miaka 38, Muislamu Katibu wa Idara ya Utawala, Chake Chake, Pemba.
33. Naaman Marshed Khamis El-Harussy, Mtanzania, Miaka 26, Muislamu, Tax driver wa Madungu, Chake Chake, Pemba.
34. Mohamed Said Mohamed (Mahdali) Mtanzania, Miaka 26, Muislamu, Mpiga Chapa, Azimio Press. wa Malindi, Zanzibar.
35. Abdulla Abeid Suleiman, Mtanzania, Miaka 44, Muislamu Mkulima wa Kizimbani, Zanzibar.

THE UMMA DEFENDANTS

36. Humoud Ali Abdulla Barwani, Mtanzania, Miaka 24, Muislamu Mwanajeshi, wa Baghani, Zanzibar.
37. Khamis Mosoud Khamis, Bajuni, Mtanzania, Miaka 25, Muislamu, Afisa wa Jeshi, wa Saateni, Zanzibar.
38. Salim Abdulla Saleh, Mtanzania, Miaka 53, Muislamu, Idara ya forodha, wa Killmani, Unguja.
39. Juma Mussa Juma, Bulushi, Mtanzania, Miaka 53, Muislamu, Karani wa Kajificheni, Zanzibar.
40. Abdulalrazak Mussa simai, Mwafrika, Mtanzania, Miaka 38, Muislamu, Mvuvi na Mkulima wa Jambiani, Zanzibar.
41. Mohamed Khalfan Salim Abdulla, Mtanzania, Miaka 29, Muislamu, Muuza Kabuku, Mapinduzi Bookshop, Chake Chake, Pondeani, Chake Chake Pemba.
42. Khamis Abdulla AMeir, Hinawi, Arab, Mtanzania, Miaka 42, Muislamu, MBM, Posta, Kiunga cha Wangazija, Miembeni, Unguja.
43. Ali Sultan Issa El-Isamail, Arab, Mtanzania Miaka 42, Muislamu, Mnager State Fuel (Shirika la Mafuta) wa Migombani, Zanzibar.
44. Abdulla Mohamed Salum (Kanga), Mtanzania, Miaka 30, Muislamu, Mwanajeshi wa Migombani na Kiwiwandui, Zanzibar.
45. Mohamed Aboud Mohamed (Chululu), Mngazija, Mtanzania, Miaka 24, Muislamu, Afisa wa Jeshi,wa Misufuni, Unguja.
46. Abdulrahman Abdulla Ali, Mtanzania, Miaka 25, Muislamu, Lt wa JWTZ wa Kisimani, Unguja.
47. Salim Ahmed Rashid, Mwafrika, Mtanzania, Miaka 25, Muislamu Lt wa JWTZ, wa Vuga, Zanzibar.
48. Ahmada Shafi Adam, Mngazija, Mtanzania, Miaka 31, Muislamu, Mwandishi wa magazeti (Uhuru wa The National) wa Kilimani, Unguja.
49. Ahmed Nassor Issa Mazrui, Mtanzania, Miaka 32, Muislamu, Building contractor, Pemba, Mkanjuni and Shangani, Zanzibar.
50. Hassan Said Mzee, Mngazija, Miaka 32 'wa Muislamu, Mwandishi wa gazeti ' The Standard, Tanzania, Malindi, Zanzibar.
51. Tahir Mohamed Adnan, Mngizija, Mtanzania, Miaka 36, Muislamu, Afisa wa Ardhi ma Misitu wa Darajani State Shop, Zanzibar.
52. Ali Mzee Ali, Mngazija, Mtanzania, Miaka 30, Muislamu, Mkuu wa mishahara na mambo ya Ofisi, Sirika la Nguvu za Umene, wa Mlandege, Zanzibar.
53. Ali Amran Ameir, Mwarabu, Mtanzania, Miaka 35, Muislamu, Idara ya habari, Zanzibar wa Shangani, Zanzibar.
54. Ibrahim Mohamed Hussein, ithnasheiry, Mtanzania, Miaka 21, Muislamu OKM wa Mwembetanga, Unguja.
55. Nassor Ali Abdulla, Mtanzania, Miaka 42, Muislamu, Idara ya Forodha, Unguja, wa Shangani, Unguga.
56. Abdulla Nassor Ali, Mtanzania, Miaka 24, Muislamu, Exchange/Beit al Ajaib, wa Shangani, Unguja.
57. Abdulla Nassor Ali (junior), Mwarabu, Mtanzania, Miaka 18, Muislamu, Mwanafunzi darasa la 12, Lumumba, wa Shangani, Unguja.

58. Zuhera Mohamed Gharib, Mwarabu, Mtanzania, Miaka 43, Muislamu, Mke wa Shangani,Unguja.
59. Mohamed Abdulla Ameir Hinawi, Mtanzania, Miaka 38, Muislamu, Mwanajeshi wa Vuga, Zanzibar.
60. Shaibu Hassan Bilali, MManyema, Mtanzania, Miaka 28, Muislamu, wa Mkamasini, Unguja.
61. Yusuf Mshangama, MnGazija, Mtanzania, Miaka23, Muislamu, Mwanajeshi wa Madaraka, Unjuga.
62. Ahmed Sultani Riyami, Mtanzania, Miaka 43, Muislamu, Imigrationwa Bububu, Zanzibar.
63. Alawi Tahir Mohamed (Shnatry), Mtanzania, Miaka 25, Muislamu, Mwanajeshi, wa Mwembe makumbi, Zanzibar.

Na watu wafuatao ambao ha wapo visiwani (The following are not in Zanzibar islands)

64. Abdulrahman Mohamed Babu, Mtanzania, Miaka 48, Muislamu, wa 14 Luthili road, Dar es Salaam.
65. Tahir Ali Salim (Mwarabi) Mtanzania, Miaka 32, Cashier (NBC Morogoro Road Branch) wa Mwembechai kono Morogoro Road/ Rungwe Street, Dar es Salaam.
66. Hashil Seif Hashil, Mwarabu, Busaidy, Mtanzania, Miaka 31, Muislamu, Mwanajeshi 2nd Lt Navy, wa Ukonga, Dar es Salaam.
67. Sailm Sareh Bahashwani, Mwarabu, Mtanzania, Miaka 31, Muislamu, Mwanajeshi wa Nachingwea Military Barracks.
68. Ali Yusuf Baalawi, Mtanzania, Miaka 42, Muislamu, Mwanajeshi (JWTZ) wa Lugalo Barracks, Dar es Salaam.
69. Hamed Hilal Mohamed, Mtanzania, Miaka 33, Muislamu, Ex-Kapteni Jeshini (JWTZ) wa Ilala National Housing Flats No 315 Block a Dar es Salaam.
70. Suleiman Mohamed Abdulla Sisi, Mtanzania, Miaka 29, Muislamu, Mwanajeshi wa Ilala Flats Block 12 Dar es Salaam.
71. Amour Mohamed Dugheish, Mtanzania, Miaka 29, Muislamu, Mwanajeshi wa Ukonga, Dar es Salaam.
72. Ahmed Mohamed Habib Toni, Mtanzania, Miaka 33 Muislamu, Ex-Lt (JWTZ) wa Lugalo Barracks, Area 6 House no. 34.
73. Haji Othman Haji Mpemba, Mtanzania, Miaka 33 Musilamu, Mwanajeshi wa Nachingwea Military Barracks, Dar es Salaam.
74. Saleh Abdulla, Mtanzania, Miaka 26, MUislamu, Ex-Lt (JWTZ) wa Forodhani, Mizingani, Zanzibar.
75. Abdulla Juma Khasim Baluch1, Mtanzania, Miaka 35, Muislamu, Mwanajeshi wa Lugalo Barracks, Dar es Salaam.
76. Ali Mahfoudh Mohamed, Mtanzania, Miaka 33, Mwanajeshi wa Ukonga, Dar es Salaam.
77. Ali Salim Hafidh, Mshihiri, Mtanzania, Miaka 32, Muislamu, Mwanajeshi wa Ukonga, Dar es Salaam.

THE UMMA DEFENDANTS

78. Shabani Salim Mbarak Nne-Nne, Mtanzania, Miaka 32, Muislamu, Mwanajeshi P.1100 Lt wa Ukonga, Dar es Salaam.
79. Badru Said Hadharmy, Mtanzania, Miaka 31, Muislamu, Research Manager NBC wa Clock Tower Branch Building, Dar es Salaam.
80. Ali Mohamed Ali Nabwa, Mngazija, Mtanzania, Miaka 37, Publicjer wa Plot 308, Block 456, Kijitonyama Dar es Salaam.
81. Abdulaziz Abdulkadir Ahmed, Mtanzania, Bujuni Mgunya, Miaka 43, Techincal Assistant, Regional wa Mindu street, Plot 563.

Charge (Section and decree) SHATAKA: Uhaini Kinyume na Kifungu ch 26 Sheria ya Jinai, Mlango 13

13. Mohamed Saki Mtendeni
14. Rashid Mohammed Ahmed Fallahy
15. Said Salim Said Baesi
16. Nurbhai Issa Nurbhai
17. Mohammed Ali Ladha
18. Abdulla Mussa Mohammed
19. Ali Hamed Hamoud Karkoboy
20. Ibrahim Omar Soud
21. Khamis Abeid Omar
22. Mohammed Khalif Mohammed
23. Naaman Narshed Khamis
24. Hamoud Ali Abdulla
25. Juma Mussa Juma
26. Khamis Abdulla Ameir
27. Ali Sultan Issa
28. Salim Ahmed Rashid (Lord Hume)
29. Ibrahim Mohamed

Waliotiwa hatianina kupelekwa mafunzoni

(List of those who have been sentenced to be sent to reformatory institutions – after the revolution Karume decided that prisons were to be called reformatory institutions.)

44.	Said Mohammed Said	Miaka 15
45.	Mohamed Abdulla Suleiman Saghir	Miaka 15
46.	Rashid Mohamed Rashid	Miaka 15
47.	Seif Said Hamed	Miaka 15
48.	Khamis Masoud Khamis	Miaka 15
49.	Salim Abdulla Saleh	Miaka 15
50.	Mohamed Khalfan Salim	Miaka 15
51.	Abdulla Mhamed Salim Kanga	Miaka 15
52.	Mohamed Aboud Mohamed Chululu	Miaka 15
53.	Mohamed Abdulla Ameir	Miaka 15
54.	Alawi Tahir Mohamed	Miaka 15
55.	Saleh Ali Saleh	Miaka 10
56.	Mohamed Ali Seif	Miaka 10
57.	Mohamed Said Mohamed Mahdali	Miaka 10
58.	Tahir Mohamed Adnan	Miaka 10

Walioachiwa na mahakama hawana makosa

(Those who have no case to answer and have been released by the Court)

59. Yusuf Ramadhan
60. Mohamed Salim Suleiman
61. Husein Mbaruk Kombo
62. Abdulla Abeid Suleiman
63. Abdulrahaman Abdulla Ali
64. Ahmada Shafi Adam
65. Hassan Said Mzee
66. Ali Mzee Ali
67. Ali Amran Ameir
68. Shibu Hassan Bilal
69. Yusuf Mshengana
70. Ahmed Sultan (Riyami)

Dar es Salaam

71. Ali Yusuf Baalawi
72. Saleh Abdulla
73. Ali Mohamed Nadwa
74. Abdulaziz Abulkadir Ahmed

Walioachiwa hawakuhitajiwa kujitetea

(Those who have no obligation to defend themselves and have been released)
75. Mohamed Abdulla Seif Panya
76. Ahmed Nassor Issa
77. Nassor Ali Abdulla
78. Abdulla Nassor Ali
79. Abdulla Nassor Ali (junior)
80. Zheira Mohamed Gharib

Aliyekufa kabla ya hukumu

(The person who died before being sentenced)
82. Abbas Mohamed Ahmed

30-43 Washitakiwa waliokuwa Dar es Salaam
Mrajis 99/76, 6 Oktoba 1976, Mwanasheria Mukuu, Zanzibar. **RUFANI NO, 1 YA ! 1974 KUTOKANA NA RUFANI NAM. 2 YA 1974 YA KORTIKUU**, Zanzibar (Registrar 99/79, 6. October 1976

Attorney General, Appeal No, 1 of 1974, From an Appeal No. 2 of 1974 of the High Court).

KUTOKANA NA KESI YA JINAI NAM. 292/73 YA MAHAKAMA YA WANACHI VUGA ZANZIBAR.

MSHTAKI........................JAMAHURI
Versus
AHMED BADAWI, QULLATEIN NA 38 WENGINE...WAOMBA RUFAANI

Nakuletea nakala za maombi ya Rufaani mbele ya Baraza la Juu ya waombaji wafuato

(From criminal case No. 292/73 of the Peoples Court of Vuga, Zanzibar.
Accuser..........Republic
Versus
Ahmed Badawi Qulatein and 38 others Appeallants.

THE UMMA DEFENDANTS

I present to you the articles submitted to Higher Organ by the following Appellants)

1. Ahmed Badawi Qullatein
2. Ali Mshangama Issa
3. Amar Salim Saada (kuku)
4. Mirajo Mpatani
5. Abdulla Ali Khamis
6. Hassan Makame Seif
7. Mohamed Abdulla (Baramia)
8. Is-Haak Haji Juma Harakati
9. Mohamed Said Mohamed (Mtendeni)
10. Rashid Mohamed Ahamed (Falahi)
11. Mussa Shaban
12. Said Salum Said (Baes)
13. Saleh Ali Saleh
14. Nurbhai Issa Nurbhai
15. Karidia Mnyeji Abdulla
16. Haroud Muhamed Salim
17. Said Mohamed Said
18. Mohamed Ali Ladha
19. Abdulla Mussa Mohamed
20. Ali Hemed Hamoud
21. Ibrahim Omar Said
22. Khamis Abeid Omar
23. Mohamed Kelef Mohamed
24. Mohamed Ali Seif
25. Naaman Marshed
26. Mohamed Said Mohamed (Mahadaly)
27. Hamoud Ali Abdulla
28. Khamis Masoud Khamis
29. Salim Abdulla Saleh
30. Juma Mussa Juma
31. Abdulrazak Mussa Simai
32. Mohamed Khelfan Salim
33. Khamis Abdulla Ameir
34. Ali Sultan Issa
35. Abdulla Mohamed Salum (Khanga)

Maelezo yamekosekana (Explanation missing)

1.	Ahmed Badawi Qullatain	Kifo*	Kifo
2.	Ali Mshangama Issa	Kifo	Kifo
3.	Amar Salim Kuku	Kifo	Kifo
4.	Miraji Mpatani	Kifo	Kifo
5.	Abdulla Ali Khasi	Kifo	Kifo
6.	Hassan Makame Seif	Kifo	Kifo
7.	Mohamed Abdulla Baramia	Kifo	Kifo
8.	Is-Haak Haji Juma Harakati	Kifo	Kifo
9.	Mohamed Said Mtendeni	Kifo	Kifo
10.	Rashid Mohamed Fallahi	Kifo	Kifo
11.	Mussa Shaban Khatif	Kifo	Kifo
12.	Said Salim Baes	Kifo	Miaka* 14
13.	Saleh Ali Saleh	Miaka 10	Miaka 10
14.	Nurbhai Issa Nurbhai	Kifo	Kifo
15.	Kadiriya Mnyeji	Kifo	Miaka 15
16.	Harub Mohamed	Kifo	Kifo
17.	Said Mohamed Said	Miaka 15	Miaka 15
18.	Mohamed Ali Ladha	Kifo	Miaka 14
19.	Abdulla Mussa Mohamed	Kifo	Miaka 9
20.	Ali Hemed Karikaboy	Kifo	Miaka 12
21.	Ibrahim Omar Soud	Kifo	Miaka 9

22.	Khamis Abeid Omar	Kifo	Miaka 9
23.	Mohamed Khelef Mohamed	Kifo	Miaka 10
24.	Mohamed Ali Seif	Miaka 10	Atoke 6/4/76
25.	Naman Marshed	Kif	Miaka 6
26.	Mohamed Said Mohamed	Miaka 10	Miaka 10
27.	Hamoud Ali Abdulla	Kifo	Miaka 18
28.	Khamis Masoud	Miaka 15	Miaka 15
29.	Salim Abdulla Saleh	Miaka 15	Miaka 10
30.	Juma Issa Juma	Kifo	Miaka 18
31.	Abdulrazak Mussa	Kifo	Miaka 6
32.	Mohamed Khalfani Salim	Miaka 15	Kifo
33.	Khamis Abdulla Ameir	Kifo	Kifo
34.	Ali Sultan Issa	Kifo	Miaka 15
35.	Abdulla Mohamed Salim	Miaka 15	Miaka 15
36.	Mohamed Aboud Chululu	Miaka 15	Miaka 18
37.	Salim Ahmed Rashid	Kifo	Miaka 15
38.	Ibrahim Mohamed Hussein	Kifo	Miaka 7
39.	Alawi Tahir	Miaka 7	Miaka 7

MRAJIS KORTI KUU
UNJUGA

Note:
* death
** number of years

Notes

Chapter 1

1 Some 23,000 slaves were being transported from Zanzibar by the mid-1860s – although this is still less than half the annual average of the Atlantic slave trade over 200 years. See Hickman, Sheriff and Alibhai-Brown (2010: 180).
2 Middle peasants, like rich peasants, are farmers who either own all their land, or own a part of it and rent the rest. However, rich peasants own more land and better agricultural implements, and while middle peasants derive their income mainly from their own labour and do not in general exploit others, rich peasants rely in part or wholly on exploitation, either by hiring in labour or by renting out land.
3 An article in *Al Falaq* on 23 September 1953 declared that 'a common roll ... irrespective of communal interests ... is what is wanted by the Zanzibari nation .... It is said we have not yet achieved the status for true representation. How absurd!' (National Archives of Zanzibar).
4 Soon after his return to Zanzibar, Babu also became the East Africa correspondent of the New China News Agency Xinhua.
5 Some Umma Party members subsequently changed their political allegiance, the best known being Salim Ahmed Salim, who joined CCM and held a string of high-ranking posts in the Tanzanian government.

Chapter 3

1 The Group of 77 is the largest intergovernmental organization of countries of the global South in the United Nations. It provides the means for countries of the South to articulate and promote their collective economic interests and enhance their joint negotiating capacity on all major international economic issues within the United Nations system, and promote South–South cooperation for development.

Chapter 4

1 Babu regarded the development of productive forces as centrally important, and in countries like Tanzania where these were at a low level, he argued that they must be developed as a priority over even the relations of production (Babu, [1982b] 2002).

NOTES

Chapter 5

1 Hamed was sent to Tabora together with Salim Saleh, Ahmed Mohamed Habibi (Tony) and Yussuf Baalway. The Nachingwea group consisted of Shaaban Salim, Suleiman Mohamed (Sisi), Amour Dugheishi, Abdulla Juma and Haji Othman.

Chapter 6

1 Babu is referring to Lenin's description of a radical newspaper as a 'collective organizer'. which may be likened to the scaffolding round a building under construction because it marks the contours of the structure and facilitates communication between builders, enabling them to distribute the work and to view the common results achieved by their organized labour.

Chapter 7

1 See 'The Indian land grab in Africa' (GOI Monitor, 2012) (Kravnicek, 2012).
2 Heritage Oil's owner and CEO is Tony Buckingham, who was once a mercenary fighter. He is now a significant donor to the UK Conservative Party.
3 The United States is also particularly concerned about the hegemony of the US dollar and anxious about the fact that China is shifting some of its foreign holdings into gold and away from the dollar, undermining its role as the world's reserve currency. See US Embassy (2009k).
4 As the *New York Times* reported (Jacobs, 2012), there is at the same time a so-called soft-power offensive, with China's media expanding in Africa and providing a new point of view to people who had long suffered a diet comprising mainly the Voice of America and the BBC.

Chapter 8

1 It was in Yemen that in September 2011, US drones targeted and killed US citizens Anwar Awlaki and Samir Khan. Two weeks later, in circumstances that have remained unexplained, Awalaki's 16-year-old son Abdulrahman, another US citizen, was also killed in a drone strike. It has been claimed that President Obama is to be vested with the power to target his own citizens for execution without any charges or due process, far from any battlefield (Greenwald, 2013).
2 These attacks were staged simultaneously in Nairobi and Dar es Salaam, and killed hundreds of people. They are believed to have been revenge for US involvement in the extradition, and alleged torture, of four members of the Egyptian Islamic Jihad arrested in Albania.

NOTES

3 As Mahmood Mamdani writes:

> In the past decade Western powers have created a political and legal structure for intervention in other wise independent countries. Key to this infrastructure [is the] United National Security Council .... The Security Council identifies states guilty of committing 'crimes against humanity'and sanctions intervention as part of a 'responsibility to protect' civilians. Third parties, other states armed to the teeth, are then free to carry out the intervention without accountability to anyone, including the Security Council.
>
> (Mamdani, 2011)

4 As Dershowitz and Paul note, 'At the same time, however, Council members have failed to act on other serious maritime crimes in the same waters – foreign fishing vessels that have stolen Somalia's rich marine resources, as well as foreign ships that have dumped toxic wastes off Somalia's shores' (2012).

5 Karume here is Amani Abeid Karume, the son of Abeid Amani Karume, the first president of Zanzibar, and himself president of Zanzibar from 2000 to 2010. According to the United States he was not keen on reconciliation because of 'historical sensitivities as son of the revolution' (US Embassy, 2009l).

6 In fact, the Permanent Voters Register vastly favoured the CCM. In the 2005 elections just before polls opened the CUF secretariat was given a makeshift list which was neither alphabetic nor had constituencies listed, and this was the only list available several years later.

References

Abdulraheem, Tajudeen (1996) 'Remembering A. M. Babu', *Review of African Political Economy*, 69: 337.

African Oil Policy Initiative Group (AOPIG) (2002) 'African oil: a priority for US national security and African development', www.israeleconomy.org/strategic/africawhitepaper.pdf (accessed February 16, 2013).

Ali, Tariq (2002) *The Clash of Fundamentalisms: Crusades, jihads and modernity*. London: Verso.

Amnesty International (1978) Report, on fiche B3. Amnesty International Archives.

Amnesty International (1979) 'The death penalty, survey by country: Tanzania'. Extract ACT 05/003/1979, on fiche A1. Amnesty International archives.

Ayani, Samuel G. (1970) *A History of Zanzibar: A study in constitutional development, 1934–1964*. Nairobi: East African Literature Bureau.

Baaz, Maria (2005) *The Paternalism of Partnership: A postcolonial reading of identity in development aid*. London: Zed.

Babu, A. M. (1967) 'The meaning of self reliance', *The Nationalist*, May 19.

Babu, A. M. ([1971] 2002) 'Postscript to how Europe underdeveloped Africa', in Salma Babu and Amrit Wilson (eds), *The Future that Works: Selected writings of A. M. Babu*. Trenton: Africa World Press.

Babu, A. M. (1975) Letter from Ukonga Prison, Tanzania to the Chairman, United Nations Commission for Human Rights, Geneva, July 1, unpublished.

Babu, A. M. (1976) Letter to Barbara Haq from Ukonga Prison, Tanzania, 25 December, unpublished.

Babu, A. M. (1981) *African Socialism or Socialist Africa*. London: Zed.

Babu, A. M. ([1981] 2002) 'The Tanzania that might have been', in Salma Babu and Amrit Wilson (eds), *The Future that Works: Selected writings of A. M. Babu*. Trenton: Africa World Press.

Babu, A. M. ([1982b] 2002) 'Introduction: University of Dar es Salaam debate on class state and imperialism' in Salma Babu and Amrit Wilson (eds), *The Future that Works: Selected writings of A.M. Babu*. Trenton: Africa World Press.

Babu, A. M. ([1982a] 2002) 'Letter to Karim Essack', in Salma Babu and Amrit Wilson (eds), *The Future that Works: Selected writings of A. M. Babu*. Trenton: Africa World Press.

Babu, A. M. ([1987a] 2002) 'China and Africa: can we learn from each other?' in Salma Babu and Amrit Wilson (eds), *The Future that Works: Selected writings of A.M. Babu*. Trenton: Africa World Press.

REFERENCES

Babu, A. M. ([1987b] 2002) 'Patrice Lumumba', in Salma Babu and Amrit Wilson (eds), *The Future that Works: Selected writings of A. M. Babu*. Trenton: Africa World Press.

Babu, A. M. (1989) 'Introduction' to Amrit Wilson, *US Foreign Policy and Revolution: The creation of Tanzania*. London: Pluto Press.

Babu, A. M. (1991) 'The 1964 revolution: lumpen or vanguard?' in Abdul Sheriff and Ed Ferguson (eds), *Zanzibar Under Colonial Rule*. London: James Curry.

Babu, A. M. ([1993] 2002) 'Third world concerns about humanitarian interventions', in Salma Babu and Amrit Wilson (eds), *The Future that Works: Selected writings of A. M. Babu*. Trenton: Africa World Press.

Babu, A. M. ([1994] 2002) 'Aid perpetuates dependency', in Salma Babu and Amrit Wilson (eds), *The Future that Works: Selected writings of A. M. Babu*. Trenton: Africa World Press.

Babu, A. M. (1994) 'Zanzibar and the future', *Change* 2(4/5).

Babu, A. M. (1995) 'Wanted: a third force in Zanzibar politics', December, unpublished.

Babu, A.M. (1996) 'Outline of memoirs', *Review of African Political Economy*, 69: 324–33.

Bader, Zinnat (1991) 'The contradictions of merchant capital, 1840–1939', in Abdul Sheriff and Ed Ferguson (eds), *Zanzibar Under Colonial Rule*. London: James Curry.

Bariyo, N. (2012) 'Zanzibar says oil revenue deal with Tanzania to spur exploration', *Dow Jones Newswires*, www.automatedtrader.net/real-time-dow-jones/116304/ (accessed November 30, 2012).

BBC News (2002) 'Angola fines Chevron for pollution', http://news.bbc.co.uk/1/hi/business/2077836.stm (accessed November 30, 2012).

Bowles, B. D. (1991) 'The struggle for independence, 1946–1963', in Abdul Sheriff and Ed Ferguson (eds), *Zanzibar Under Colonial Rule*. London: James Curry.

Burgess, G. Thomas (2009) *Race, Revolution, and the Struggle for Human Rights in Zanzibar: The Memoirs of Ali Sultan Issa and Seif Sharif Hamad*. Athens, Oh.: Ohio University Press.

Bush, George W. (2002) *The National Security Strategy of the United States of America*, September. www.state.gov/documents/organization/63562.pdf (accessed March 20, 2013).

Cannon Lorgan, Christy (1999) *The experience of Villagisation: Lessons from Ethiopia, Mozambique, and Tanzania*. London: Oxfam.

Chachage, Chambi (2009) 'What Norway wants from Zanzibar', http://pambazuka.org/en/category/features/60746 (accessed November 30, 2012).

Channel 4 News (2011) 'US hunter-killer drones "flying from Sechelles"', www.channel4.com/news/american-hunter-killer-drones-flying-from-seychelles (accessed November 30, 2012).

Chase, H. (1976) 'The Zanzibar treason trial', *Review of African Political Economy*, 6: 14–33.

REFERENCES

Coleman, P. (2009) 'Reinforcing success: using lessons learned from foreign aid delivery to plan theatre security cooperation in Africa', Master's thesis, Joint Forces Staff College Joint Advanced Warfighting School. www.dtic.mil/cgi-bin/GetTRDoc?AD=ADA530116 (accessed November 30, 2012).

Dehghan, Saeed Kamali (2011) 'Iran "arrests 12 CIA agents"' *Guardian*, 24 November, www.guardian.co.uk/world/2011/nov/24/iran-claims-arrests-of-cia-agents (accessed November 30, 2012).

Depelchin, Jacques (1991) 'The transition from slavery, 1873–1914' in Abdul Sheriff and Ed Ferguson (eds), *Zanzibar Under Colonial Rule*. London: James Curry.

Dershowitz, Suzanne and Paul, James (2012) 'Fishermen, pirates and naval squadrons: the Security Council and the Battle over Somalia's Coastal Seas', *Global Policy Forum*, www.globalpolicy.org/images/pdfs/Security_Council/GPF_Somalia_illegal_fishing.pdf (accessed November 30, 2012).

Dira Yetu (2011) 'Zanzibar fight for more autonomy', http://dirayetu.blogspot.com/2011/07/zanzibar-fight-for-more-autonomy.html (accessed November 30, 2012).

Dodma (2012) 'Tanzania: leaders nod to union structure', *Tanzania Daily News*, http://allafrica.com/stories/201211130226.html. (accessed January 18, 2013).

Engdahl, William (2011) 'Nato's war on Libya is directed against China: AFRICOM and the threat to China's national energy security', *Global Research*, www.globalresearch.ca/index.php?context=va&aid=26763 (accessed November 30, 2012).

Free Library (2009) 'A golden example: the history of Lily Golden, a Russian African-American professor of history, is an inspiration to those fighting against supremacists worldwide', *Free Library*, www.thefreelibrary.com/A+golden+example%3A+the+history+of+Lily+Golden,+a+Russian...-a0194269703 (accessed November 30, 2012).

Glazebrook, Dan (2013) 'The West's war against African development continues', *Counterpunch*, February 15–17, www.counterpunch.org/2013/02/15/the-wests-war-against-african-development-continues/ (accessed February 16, 2013).

GOI Monitor (2012) 'The Indian land grab in Africa', *Countercurrents*, December 20, www.countercurrents.org/goi201211.htm (accessed November 30, 2012).

Greenwald, Glenn (2013) 'Chilling legal memo from Obama DOJ justifies assassination of US citizens', *Guardian*, February 5, www.guardian.co.uk/commentisfree/2013/feb/05/obama-kill-list-doj-memo (accessed March 20, 2013).

Habte Selassie, Bereket (1996) 'Abdulrahman Mohamed Babu: revolutionary democrat, journalist and statesman', *Review of African Political Economy*, 69: 333.

Hadjivayanis, George and Ferguson, Ed (1991) 'The development of a colonial working class', in Abdul Sheriff and Ed Ferguson (eds), *Zanzibar Under Colonial Rule*. London: James Curry

REFERENCES

Havnevik (1993) cited in Cannon Lorgan, Christy (1999) *The experience of Villagisation: Lessons from Ethiopia, Mozambique, and Tanzania.* London: Oxfam.

Heningsen, Patrick (2011) 'West vs China: a new cold war begins on Libyan soil', *21st Century Wire*, April 13, http://21stcenturywire.com/2011/04/12/2577/ (accessed November 30, 2012).

Hickman, J. K. (1995). Interview for British Diplomatic Oral History Programme, p. 10, www.chu.cam.ac.uk/archives/collections/BDOHP/Hickman.pdf. (accessed November 30, 2012).

Hickman, K., Sheriff, A. and Alibhai-Brown, Y. (2010) 'Debating Africa: BBC's documentary *Heart and Soul – Return to Zanzibar*', *Information, Society and Justice*, 3(2): 177–85, www.londonmet.ac.uk/fms/MRSite/acad/dass/ISJ Journal/V3N2/09_Debating Africa_BBC_Hickman, Sherrif & Alibhai-Brown.pdf (accessed March 20, 2013).

HMSO (1961) *Report: Commission of Inquiry Zanzibar Riots*, June, p. 3. London: HMSO.

Holslag, Jonathan (2009) 'China's new security strategy for Africa', *Parameters*, Summer: 23–37, www.carlisle.army.mil/usawc/parameters/Articles/09summer/holslag.pdf (accessed November 30, 2012).

HSPP (2009) *Health Sector Performance Profile Report Update: Mainland Tanzania July 2008–June 2009*, http://hdptz.esealtd.com/fileadmin/documents/Other_Health_Meetings/Health_Sector_Performance_Profile_Report_2009_4_Nov_FINAL_DRAFT.pdf (accessed April 30, 2013).

Hughes, Karen P. (2006) Remarks at the Shell Distinguished Lecture Series, http://merln.ndu.edu/archivepdf/nss/state/64106.pdf (accessed November 30, 2012).

International Labour Organization (ILO) (2011) 'Tanzania (mainland and Zanzibar) country profile', www.ilo.org/public/english/employment/ent/coop/africa/countries/eastafrica/tanzania.htm (accessed November 30, 2012).

Interights (2011) 'Case against Djibouti is first to challenge African cooperation in CIA secret detention program', International Centre for the Legal Protection of Human Rights, www.interights.org/document/9/index.html (accessed November 30, 2012).

Jacobs, A. (2012) 'Pursuing soft power, China puts stamp on Africa's news', *New York Times*, August 16, www.nytimes.com/2012/08/17/world/africa/chinas-news-media-make-inroads-in-africa.html?_r=1&pagewanted=all (accessed November 30, 2012).

Jamiiforums (2008) 'Dar es Salaam: Ukonga prison cells being prepared for "VIP" guests? Anticipated influx of high-profile prisoners charged with grand corruption', May 30, www.jamiiforums.com/jukwaa-la-siasa/16572-vip-prisons-coming-soon-in-tanzania.html (accessed November 30, 2012).

Jorgic, Razen (2012) 'Tension heats up at "spice island"', Reuters, October 16, www.stuff.co.nz/world/africa/7868174/Tension-heats-up-at-spice-island (accessed November 30, 2012).

Kaijage, Florian (2012) 'Govt in fresh Sh32bn query over Kiwira coal mine',

June 30, www.ippmedia.com/frontend/index.php/ahtml/=1?l=43172 (accessed January 16, 2013).

Kassum, Alnoor (2007) *Africa's Winds of Change: Memoirs of an international Tanzanian*. London: I.B. Tauris.

Kravnicek, Natasha (2012) 'Land acquisitions: India's investments in Africa', http://farmlandgrab.org/post/view/21193 (accessed November 30, 2012).

Kuper, Leo (1970) 'Continuities and discontinuities in race relations: evolutionary or revolutionary change', *Cahiers d'etudes africaines* 10(39): 361–83, www.persee.fr/web/revues/home/prescript/article/cea_0008-0055_1970_num_10_39_2828# (accessed March 20, 2013).

Lissu, Tundu (2002) 'Tanzania human rights advocacy and the Bulyanhulu Gold Mine', www.eli.org/pdf/advocacytoolscasestudies/casestudy.tanzania.final.pdf (accessed November 30, 2012).

Liu Guangyuan (2012) 'A mutually beneficial new type of China–Africa strategic relationship', http://ke.china-embassy.org/eng/xw/t962845.htm (accessed November 30, 2012).

Lofchie, M. F. (1965) *Zanzibar Background to Revolution*. Princeton, N.J.: Princeton University Press.

Machira, Polycarp (2012) 'Zanzibar seeks new union format', *The Citizen*, October 17, www.thecitizen.co.tz/magazines/32-political-platform/26609-zanzibar-seeks-new-union-format.html (accessed November 30, 2012).

Mamdani, Mahmood (1996) 'Babu: a personal tribute', *Review of African Political Economy*, 69: 344.

Mamdani, Mahmood (2005) *Good Muslim Bad Muslim: Islam, the USA and the global war against terror*. Delhi: Permanent Black.

Mamdani, Mahmood (2011) 'What does Gaddafi's fall mean for Africa?' *Al Jazeera*, October 26, www.aljazeera.com/indepth/opinion/2011/08/201182812377546414.html (accessed 30 April 2013).

Maoulidi, Salma (2011) 'Between law and culture, contemplating rights for women in Zanzibar', in Dorothy Hodgson (ed.). *Gender and Culture at the Limits of Rights*. Philadelphia, Pa.: University of Pennsylvania Press.

Mgamba, Richard (2012) 'How foreign miners made their fortune in Tanzania', *Guardian on Sunday*, April 1, www.ippmedia.com/frontend/index.php/as_dansi/function.fopen?l=40068 (accessed November 30, 2012).

Ministry of Labour, Youth, Children and Women Development Zanzibar (2007) Zanzibar Youth Employment Action Plan, July 2007.

Mjasiri, Jaffar (2011) 'Lesson from Zanzibar's government of national unity', *Daily News* December, www.dailynews.co.tz/feature/?n=17835 (accessed November 30, 2012).

Msoma, Salim (2011) 'Obituary: Ahmed Badawi Qullatein', November 2, Circulated by Zanzibar Institute for Research and Public Policy zirpp google group.

Munte, Lucas (2012) 'Tanzania: nation's external debt now at u.s.$9,788 million', *Africa Business Week*, June 4, http://allafrica.com/stories/201206041217.html (accessed November 30, 2012).

Mutarubukwa, Al-amani (2011) 'How multinationals conduct big rip offs', *The Citizen*, 4 December, www.thecitizen.co.tz/component/content/article/37-tanzania-top-news-story/17652-how-multinationals-conduct-big-rip-offs.html (accessed November 30, 2012).

Mutch, Thembi (2010) 'Jatropha biofuels: the true cost to Tanzania', *The Ecologist*, February 15, www.theecologist.org/trial_investigations/414648/jatropha_biofuels_the_true_cost_to_tanzania.html (accessed November 30, 2012).

Mutch, Thembi (2012) 'Who will benefit from East Africa's oil and gas?' *African Globe*, July 25, www.africanglobe.net/business/benefit-east-africas-oil-gas/ (accessed November 30, 2012).

Naluyaga, Ray (2010) 'Karume's legacy secured', *The Citizen* April 6, http://thecitizen.co.tz/magazines/32-political-platform/1144-karumes-legacy-secured.html (accessed November 30, 2012).

Napoli, Fatma Jiddawi and Saleh, Ahmed Mohamed (2005) 'The role of sexual violence against Zanzibari women in the human rights conflict with Tanzania over sovereignty', in Faye V. Harrison (ed.), *Resisting Racism and Xenophobia: Global perspectives on race, gender and human rights*. Oxford: AltaMira Press.

Mugarula, Florence (2012) 'Conflicting statements on future of the Union', *The Citizen*, November 13, www.thecitizen.co.tz/sport/37-tanzania-top-news-story/27153-conflicting-statements-on-future-of-the-union.html (accessed January 18, 2013).

Naluyaga, Ray (2010) 'Karume's legacy secured', *The Citizen*, April 6. www.thecitizen.co.tz/magazines/32-political-platform/1144-karumes-legacy-secured.html (accessed April 8, 2013).

O'Connor (1988) Cited in Cannon Lorgan, Christy (1999) *The experience of Villagisation: Lessons fromEthiopia, Mozambique, and Tanzania*. London: Oxfam.

Open Society Foundation (2013) *Globalizing Torture: CIA secret detention and extraordinary rendition*, Open Society Justice Initiative, www.opensocietyfoundations.org/sites/default/files/globalizing-torture-20120205.pdf (accessed February 10, 2013).

Pilger, John (2011) 'The Son of Africa claims the continent's crown jewels', John Pilger.com, October 20, www.johnpilger.com/articles/the-son-of-africa-claims-a-continents-crown-jewels (accessed November 30, 2012).

Pilger, John (2013) 'The untold US invasion of Africa', *Green Left*, www.greenleft.org.au/node/53202 (accessed February 10, 2013).

Platform (2010) 'A lake of oil: Congo's contracts escalate conflict, pollution and poverty', www.platformlondon.org/carbonweb/documents/drc/A_Lake_of_Oil_Congo_DRC_Tullow_PLATFORM_May_2010.pdf (accessed November 30, 2012).

Platform (2012) 'Tullow Oil's foul play in Ghana', http://ghanasoilgasdiary.blogspot.co.uk/2010/04/kosmostullow-spill-oil.html (accessed January 18, 2013).

Pomerance, Michla (1982) *Self-Determination in Law and Practice*. The Hague: Martinus Nijhoff.

REFERENCES

Press TV (2012) 'Drones from Kenya killing 30 civilians in Somalia', http://presstv.com/detail/219584.html (accessed November 30, 2012).

Public Record Office (1959) *British Intelligence Report for the month of June 1959*, CO 822, 1376, 3185867.

Public Record Office (1962a) *British Resident to Secretary of State, Zanzibar security situation 23 June*, CO 822, 2047.

Public Record Office (1962b) *Babu Sedition Trial*, January 126, PRO 2166.

Qazi, T. (2011) 'The spring revolution: age of hope and time for disappointment', *Countercurrents*, July 8, www.countercurrents.org/qazi080711.htm (accessed November 30, 2012).

Rashid, S. (2011) 'Zanzibar beyond the elections: comment on concept note by the International Law and Policy Institute (ILPI) of Oslo providing strategic transitional support for the Government of National Unity', May.

Ratio Magazine (2012) 'Legislating for the nascent oil and gas sector in the EAC: Tanzania', July, www.ratio- magazine.com/201207134126/Tanzania/Legislating-for-the-Nascent-Oil-and-Gas-Sector-in-the-EAC-Tanzania.html. (accessed November 30, 2012).

Reuters (2012) 'Zanzibar says 145 killed in the ferry disaster last week', July 22, http://allafrica.com/stories/201211130226.html (accessed January 18, 2013).

Robarge, D. S. (2008) Review of *All the Shah's men: An American coup and the roots of Middle East terror*, www.cia.gov/library/center-for-the-study-of-intelligence/csi-publications/csi-studies/studies/vol48no2/article10.html (accessed November 30, 2012).

Rowell, Andy and Eveline Lubbers (2010) 'Ken Saro-Wiwa was framed secret evidence shows', December 5, www.independent.co.uk/news/world/africa/ken-sarowiwa-was-framed-secret-evidence-shows-2151577.html (accessed January 18, 2013).

Scahill, J. (2010) 'Obama's expanding covert wars', *The Nation*, June 4, www.thenation.com/blog/obamas-expanding-covert-wars# (accessed November 30, 2012).

Sharife, K. (2009) 'Tanzania's pot of gold', *Pambazuka*, October 1, http://pambazuka.org/en/category/features/59142 (accessed November 30,2012).

Sheriff, Abdul (1991) 'The peasantry under imperialism, 1873–1963', in Abdul Sheriff and Ed Ferguson (eds), *Zanzibar Under Colonial Rule*. London: James Curry

Sheriff, Abdul (2008) 'Maritime culture and globalisation in the Indian Ocean', paper presented at ZIORI Conference on the Indian Ocean, Zanzibar, 15–17 August.

Shivji, Issa G. (2008) *Pan-Africanism or Pragmatism? Lessons of Tanganyika-Zanzibar Union*. Dar es Salaam: Mkuki na Nyota.

Smith, A (1971), RHL, East Africa, MSS.Afr.S.2250, '*Zanzibar Symposium*', tape recording of interview at Oxford University by Alison Smith, October 16, cited in G. Thomas Burgess (2003) 'Imagined generations: constructing youth in revolutionary Zanzibar', paper presented at International Conference on Youth and the Politics of Generational Conflict in Africa,

University of Leiden, www.ascleiden.nl/pdf/conference24042003-burgess. pdf (accessed November 30, 2012).

Staalesen, Atle (2012) 'Oil spill at Kharyaga', *Barents Observer*, October 8, http://barentsobserver.com/en/nature/oil-spill-kharyaga-08-10 (accessed November 30, 2012).

Stith, C. (2010) 'Radical Islam in East Africa', *Annals of the American Academy of Political Science*, http://ann.sagepub.com/content//632/1/55.full.pdf+html (accessed April 30, 2013).

Taylor, David (2009) 'Evo Morales – from poverty to power', *Labour Campaign for International Development*, December 8, http://lcid.org.uk/2009/12/08/evo/ (accessed November 30, 2012).

TDHS (2004/5) Tanzania Demographic and Health Survey, www.measuredhs.com/pubs/pdf/FR173/FR173-TZ04-05.pdf (accessed May 15, 2013).

Tradingeconomics (2013) 'Mortality rate: infant (per 1000 live births) in Bolivia', www.tradingeconomics.com/bolivia/mortality-rate-infant-per-1-000-live-births-wb-data.html (accessed May 15, 2013).

US Department of Defense (2012) 'Sustaining global leadership: priorities for 21st century defense', January 3, www.defense.gov/news/Defense_Strategic_Guidance.pdf (accessed November 30, 2012).

US Embassy (2005a) 'Zanzibar's imams declare a truce', cable, http://leaks.hohesc.us/?view=05DARESSALAAM1015 (accessed November 30, 2012).

US Embassy (2005b) 'Whither Tanzania, charges end of tour reflections', cable, http://wikileaks.org/cable/2005/07/05DARESSALAAM1307.html (accessed November 30, 2012).

US Embassy (2006a) 'Iran: Tanzania believes more diplomatic efforts, working through IAEA needed before reporting to UNSC', cable, www.wikileaks.org/cable/2006/01/06DARESSALAAM125.html (accessed November 30, 2012).

US Embassy (2006b) 'Ghosts of revolution haunt Zanzibar's reconciliation process', cable, www.wikileaks.org/cable/2006/08/06DARESSALAAM1433.html#par1 (accessed November 30, 2012).

US Embassy (2006c) 'Overflights: help us do it ourselves', www.cablegatesearch.net/cable.php?id=06DARESSALAAM771&q=counter%20terrorism (accessed November 30, 2012).

US Embassy (2007a) 'Zanzibar: Tanzanian foreign minister updates Ambassador Retzer on reconciliaton efforts', cable, www.cablegatesearch.net/cable.php?id=07DARESSALAAM609 (accessed November 30, 2012).

US Embassy (2007b) 'Tanzania walks fine line on Iran's nuclear program', cable, http://wikileaks.org/cable/2007/12/07DARESSALAAM1568.html (accessed November 30, 2012).

US Embassy (2007c) 'Islamic radicals block American Muslims from evening prayers', cable, www.cablegatesearch.net/cable.php?id=07DARESSALAAM894 (accessed November 30, 2012).

US Embassy (2008a) 'Zanzibar primer: the issue, why it matters & what we are doing about it', cable, http://wikileaks.org/cable/2008/07/08DARESSALAAM444.html (accessed November 30, 2012).

US Embassy (2008b) 'Tanzania: investment climate statement 2008', cable,

REFERENCES

www.scoop.co.nz/stories/WL0801/S00439.htm (accessed November 30, 2012).

US Embassy (2008c) 'Update on Tanzania terrorist issues', cable, www.cablegatesearch.net/cable.php?id=08DARESSALAAM91 (accessed November 30, 2012).

US Embassy (2009a) 'Scenesetter for Deputy Secretary Lew visit to Tanzania', cable, www.scoop.co.nz/stories/WL0906/S00788.htm (accessed November 30, 2012).

US Embassy (2009b) 'Zanzibar: ruling party thinking', cable, http://dazzlepod.com/cable/09DARESSALAAM130/ (accessed November 30, 2012).

US Embassy (2009c) 'Tanzania 2009 investment climate statement', cable, www.scoop.co.nz/stories/WL0901/S00583.htm (accessed November 30, 2012).

US Embassy (2009d) 'President Kikwete rallies Zanzibar CCM party supporters but shrugs off reconciliation', cable, www.cablegatesearch.net/cable.php?id=09DARESSALAAM54 (accessed November 30, 2012).

US Embassy (2009e) 'Zanzibar opposition CUF thinking', cable, www.cablegatesearch.net/cable.php?id=09DARESSALAAM123 (accessed November 30, 2012).

US Embassy (2009f) 'Zanzibar: donors seek common position on elections, political reconciliation', cable, www.cablegatesearch.net/cable.php?id=09DARESSALAAM385 (accessed November 30, 2012).

US Embassy (2009g) 'Zanzibar: Karume berates ambassadors on joint statement', cable, www.cablegatesearch.net/cable.php?id=09DARESSALAAM578 (accessed November 30, 2012).

US Embassy (2009h) 'Zanzibar opposition leader against violence but offers no new ideas', cable, www.cablegatesearch.net/cable.php?id=09DARESSALAAM628 (accessed November 30, 2012).

US Embassy (2009i) 'Tanzania oil and gas exploration: oil unlikely, gas needs investment and government action', cable, http://wikileaks.org/cable/2009/06/09DARESSALAAM368.html (accessed November 30, 2012).

US Embassy (2009j) 'Tanzania and Iran sign defense mou', cable, http://wikileaks.org/cable/2009/01/09DARESSALAAM60.html (accessed November 30, 2012).

US Embassy (2009k) 'Media reaction: US–China–Japan relations, US policy', cable, http://wikileaks.org/cable/2009/04/09BEIJING1134.html# (accessed November 30, 2012).

US Embassy (2009l) 'Tanzanian home minister hints about national views', cable, http://wikileaks.org/cable/2009/01/09DARESSALAAM63.html (accessed November 30, 2012).

US Embassy (2010a) 'East African legislature could be vehicle for U.S. regional goals', cable, www.cablegatesearch.net/cable.php?id=10DARESSALAAM88 (accessed November 30, 2012).

US Embassy (2010b) 'East African Community Sec-Gen on USG-EAC cooperation', cable, www.cablegatesearch.net/cable.php?id=10DARESSALAAM105 (accessed November 30, 2012).

REFERENCES

US Embassy (2010c) 'TPDF past, present and future from the optic of the US Defense attaché ', cable, www.cablegatesearch.net/cable.php?id=10 DARESSALAAM114 (accessed November 30, 2012).

US Joint Chiefs of Staff (2008) 'Civil military operations', Publication 3-57, www.fas.org/irp/doddir/dod/jp3_57.pdf (accessed November 30, 2012).

US State Department (2001–09) 'About us', US State Department Archive, http://2001-2009.state.gov/s/ct/about/index.htm (accessed January 18, 2013).

Wateraid (2011) Core information, www.wateraid.org/uk/what_we_do/where_we_work/tanzania/ (accessed November 30, 2012).

Williams, Selina (2012) 'Statoil upbeat on "hot" East African prospects' *Dow Jones Newswires,* November 14, www.rigzone.com/news/oil_gas/a/122099/Statoil_Upbeat_on_Hot_East_African_Prospect. (accessed November 30, 2012).

Wilson, Amrit (1987) 'Putting the fix on Zanzibar', *South*, April: 113.

Wilson, Amrit (1989) *US Foreign Policy and Revolution: The creation of Tanzania.* London: Pluto Press.

World Bank and International Monetary Fund (IMF) (1992) Africa Strategy for Mining, technical paper. Washington DC: World Bank.

World Food Program (2004/2005) 'Tanzania demographic and health survey' in Tanzania Overview, www.wfp.org/countries/Tanzania--United-Republic-Of/Overview (accessed November 30, 2012).

Yi-Chong, X. (2008) 'China and the United States in Africa: coming conflict or commercial coexistence', *Australian Journal of International Affairs*, 62(1): 16–3.

Yussuf, Issa (2012) 'Tanzania: Zanzibar minister relieved of duties', *Daily News*, October 17, http://dailynews.co.tz/index.php/local-news/10608-zanzibar-minister-relieved-of-duties (accessed November 30, 2012).

Zakaria, M. (2012) 'Zanzibar separatist group leaders charged with inciting murder', Reuters, October 22, www.reuters.com/article/2012/10/22/us-tanzania-zanzibar-separatists-idUSBRE89L0XR20121022 (accessed March 20, 2013).

ZaNews (1963) 'Report of Conference of All Zanzibar Students' Association', September 17–26, 1963.

Zanzinet forum, www.zanzinet.org/zanzibar/economy/utangulizi.html (accessed November 30, 2012).

Zanzibar Committee for Democracy (2005) *Zanzibar Election Watch*, www.zanzinet.org/files/Zanzibar_Elections_Watch_6.pdf (accessed November 30, 2012).

Index

A
Abdi, Abdirahim, 120, 121
Abdulraheem, Tajudeen, 98, 99
Africa Kwetu, 44
African Charter, 115
African Commission on Human and People's Rights, 8
African National Congress (ANC), 95
African Oil Policy Initiative Group (AOPIG), 111
African Socialism, 72, 73
African Socialism or Socialist Africa, 95
AFRICOM, 6, 111, 118, 120, 121
Afro-Shirazi Party (ASP), 3, 17,19, 25, 26, 27, 28, 29, 30, 31, 32, 33, 34, 35, 37, 38, 39, 42, 43, 44, 45, 46, 47, 49, 52, 54, 55, 56, 57, 58, 61, 77, 80, 81, 82, 83, 87, 90, 92, 93, 95, 100
aid, 55, 64, 68, 71, 73, 102, 103, 106–7, 129
Al-Asad, 114, 115
Al-Shabaab, 7, 8
Algeria, 2, 11, 20, 23, 25, 85, 111, 115
Ali Muhsin, 17, 28, 29, 36, 37, 43, 46
Ali, Mzee Ali, 102, 151, 154
Ali, Tahir, 93, 96, 97, 152
All-African People's Conference, 27, 28
Ameir, Khamis, 24, 25, 36, 37, 40, 43, 49, 54, 55, 56, 65, 80, 83, 84, 91, 92, 94, 136
Amin, Samir, 20
AngloGold Ashanti (AGA), 104
Angola, 69, 85, 119, 130
Anti Terrorism Assistance (ATA), 116
Arusha Declaration, 72–4, 103

Association for Islamic Mobilisation and Propagation (AIMP), 132, 133, 135
Attwood, William, 62, 65

B
Babu, Abdulrahman Mohamed, 12, 19–21, 40, 44, 48, 49, 50, 66, 80, 82, 93, 95–7, 98, 99
and All African People's Conference, 28–9
and Che Guevara, 53
and early days of People's Republic of Zanzibar, 53–4
economic policies, 58–60, 71–6
and launch of Umma Party, 42
and Malcolm X, 67–8
and mass party against colonialism, 20, 21–3
and Pan-Africanism, 20, 25, 27–9, 42, 67, 98, 140
relationship with China, 5, 20, 59, 68–71, 157
sedition charge against, 36–9
and the Treason Trial, 83, 85, 86, 90–3
and the Union of Zanzibar and Tanganyika, 60, 64
US fears of, 52, 61–2
and Zanzibar of the future, 135–7
Badawi, Qullatein, 24, 25, 37, 40, 44, 78, 92, 136
Bakari, Seif, 79, 83, 93
Banda, Hastings, 29
Baramia, Mohamed Abdulla, 24, 155
Barrick Gold, 104
biofuel, 106
Bolivia, 122, 135
Botswana, 120

INDEX

Brunei, 133
Bulyanhulu, 104
Burundi, 94, 120, 121

C

Cameroon, 28, 119
Canada, 101, 106, 127
Carlucci, Frank, 4, 52, 64, 68
Central Intelligence Agency (CIA), 3, 4, 8, 26, 52, 61, 64, 112
    day to day liaison with, 64
    prisons, 114, 115
Chad, 56, 116
Chama cha Mapinduzi (CCM), 1, 100, 125
    and oil, 128, 130
    and Uamsho, 133
Chama cha Mapinduzi (CCM) Zanzibar, 100, 101, 102, 109, 125, 126, 131, 132, 133, 134, 137, 157, 159
China, 5, 26, 31, 38, 55, 59, 68
    and AFRICOM, 6, 111
    British fears of, 17
    as an inspiration for anti-colonial struggle, 5
    nationalism and socialism of, 20
    News Agency, 37
    socialist revolution of, 20
    and TAZARA, 68–70
    trade agreements with, 69
    US fears of, 5, 110, 111
Chiume, Kanyama, 29
Citizen Dialogue Program, 123
Civic United Front (CUF), 1, 100, 101, 102, 124, 125, 126, 127, 128, 129, 130, 131, 132, 133, 159
cloves, 12, 13, 14, 59, 81
Colito barracks, 51
colonialism, 2, 11, 16, 22, 23, 32, 42
    Belgian, 28
    break completely from, 59
    early struggles against, 15
    mass party against, 20, 22
    and racial conflict, 13

counterterrorism, 8, 115, 116, 120, 122, 125
Cuba, 2, 36, 38, 54, 78
'Cuba of Africa', 4, 52

D

Democratic Republic of Congo (DRC), 108
Department for International Development (DfID), 102, 127
Djibouti, 114
Dourado, Wolfgang, 84, 91, 92
Dugeshi, Amour, 48, 93, 152
Duni, Juma, 127, 129, 130

E

East African Community, 119–20
East African Currency Board, 129
Ebrahim, Gora, 63
Economic Exclusive Zone, 109
environmental damage, 130
Essack, Karim, 34, 58
exploitation
    of 'dwindling natural resources' by the USA, 119
    and SEZs, 105
    of surplus value from labour, 104, 105
    of Tanzania's coal and iron ore, 75
    of Zanzibar's oil, 108

F

Fanon, Frantz, 28
Federation of Progressive Trade Unions (FPTU), 25, 36, 37, 42, 43
Freedom Committee, 27, 29, 31

G

Gaddafi, Muammar, 2,
Geita mine, 104
Ghana, 11, 12, 20, 27, 104, 130
Government of National Unity, 1, 8, 101, 123, 125, 126, 127, 128, 129, 130, 131, 132, 133

INDEX

Group of 77, 54, 157
Guevara, Che, 53, 54

H
Habte Selassie, Bereket, 28
Hadi, Sheikh Farid, 133
Hamad, Seif Sharif, 101, 124, 127
Hanga, Abdullah, 49, 66, 67, 80, 81
Hashil Seif Hashil, 3, 47, 48, 80, 83, 87, 88, 93, 97, 136
Heritage Oil, 108, 158
Hilal, Hamed, 22, 24, 36, 78, 79, 80, 83, 85, 86, 87, 88, 93, 96, 97
Himid, Yusuf, 79, 131, 134
humanitarian intervention, 7, 117
Huntington, Samuel, 117

I
Iddi, Seif Ali, 113, 131
Indian National Association, 26, 32
Indonesia, 59, 60, 64
Interights, 8, 114, 115
International Confederation of Free Trade Union (ICFTU), 25, 26
International Law and Policy Institute (ILPI), 130
International Monetary Fund (IMF), 98, 103, 104, 134
Iran, 7, 13, 112, 113, 122,
Issa, Ali Sultan, 24, 36, 37, 49, 80, 92

J
Juma, Abdulla, 36, 93, 97,152, 157
Jumbe, Aboud, 46, 49, 66, 83, 87, 90, 96
Jusa, Ismail, 127, 129, 134

K
Karume 1, 3, 16, 17, 18, 19, 27, 29, 30, 31, 37, 39, 46, 49, 50, 52, 54, 55, 57, 58, 61, 62, 64, 65, 66
  assassination of, 82, 83
  and Committee of Fourteen, 79, 80, 81
  despotic rule of, 77–82
  funeral of, 85,
  and judicial system, 57, 81
  'plot' against, 82
Kaunda, Kenneth, 29
Kawawa, Rashidi, 30, 66, 70, 71, 85
Kenya, 2, 3, 4, 7, 8, 16, 25, 30, 44, 46, 47, 51, 52, 61, 62, 63, 65, 109, 116, 119, 120, 125, 129
Kenyatta, Jomo, 46, 52, 63
Kikwete, Jakaya, 8,113, 115, 121, 124, 125, 126, 127, 128, 129
Kotecha, Kanti, 38

L
Lancaster House Conference, 39, 40, 42, 56,
land reform, 39, 40
landowners, 13, 14, 17, 19, 26, 27, 31
laws
  labour laws in Tanzania, 105
  regarding oil exploration, 109
  and rendition, 114
  sedition, 38
  in Zanzibar, 43, 44, 56, 57, 65, 77, 84
Lenhardt, Alfonso, 102, 120, 121
Leonhart, William, 61, 62, 65, 66
liberation movements, 26, 28, 63, 69
Libya, 2, 6, 7, 107, 111
Lumumba, Patrice, 4, 28, 52
Lumumbaist, 95

M
Mahfoudh, Ali, 45, 79, 93, 96, 97, 152
Malawi, 21, 89, 94, 115
Malcolm X, 67, 68
Mamdani, Mahmood, 48, 122, 123, 158
Mau Mau, 16, 25
Membe, Bernard, 125
Mfaune, Mohamed, 54, 55
Milner, Ralph, 38
Mkapa, Benjamin, 103, 104, 107, 114
Mnyeji, Kadiria, 24, 150, 155

Moumie, Felix Roland, 28
Movimento Popular de Libertação de Angola (MPLA), 95
Moyo, Hasan Nassor, 49, 56, 66, 87, 88, 134
Mpatani, Miraji, 92, 155
Msoma, Salim, 24
Mtwara, 110
Mukandala, Rwekaza, 124, 125
multiracial, 17, 41, 42
Mulamula, Liberata, 112, 113
Mushingi, Tulinabo, 108, 109, 127
Mwamunyange, Davis, 121
Mwapachu, Juma, 121
Mwinyi, Ali Hassan, 103, 113

N
NASA (National Aeronautics and Space Administration), 26, 47
Nasser, Gamal Abdel, 2, 36
nationalization, 59, 75, 76
Netherlands, the, 101, 106, 127
Niger, 108, 111, 119, 131, 133
Nkomo, Joshua, 29
Nkrumah, Kwame, 20, 28, 63
Non-Proliferation Treaty (NPT), 112
Norway, 101, 108, 127, 128, 134
Nyerere, Julius, 1, 3, 4, 18, 29, 30, 31, 46, 50, 51
 and China, 71–6
 and Colito Mutiny, 52, 56, 62–4
 economic policies of, 81, 82
 and human rights, 86– 91, 96, 103, 126
 progressive cult of, 64–6

O
Obama, Barack, 7, 8, 111, 122, 158
Obote, Milton, 52
Open Society Foundation, 115
Organisation of African Unity (OAU), 64, 67, 82, 85, 95
Othman, Haji, 93, 97, 152, 157

P
Palestine, 23

Pan African Freedom Movement of East and Central Africa (PAFMECA), 27, 29, 30
Pan-Africanism, 20, 42, 63, 98, 140
Pan Africanist Congress, 63, 95
Party of National Unity for the Sultan's Subjects (PNUSS), 16, 17
peasants, 14, 16, 17, 18, 22, 26, 31, 32, 58, 73, 75, 157
Picard, Frederick, 55
preventive detention, 57, 65, 85
productive forces, 8, 76

R
racial conflict/tension 14, 15, 26, 27, 31, 33, 34, 35, 56, 90,
racial representation, 17
Rashid, Salim, 24, 234
rendition, 6, 8, 114, 115, 119
Research and Education for Democracy in Tanzania (REDET), 124, 125
Retzer, Michael, 115, 116, 124, 125
Riami, Eddy, 134
Rusk, Dean, 50, 52
Rwanda, 48, 120, 121,

S
Saadalla, Saleh, 44, 49, 78
Salim, Ahmed Salim, 24, 157
Salim, Amar (Kuku), 24, 149, 155
Salim, Shaaban, 22, 24, 36, 78, 79, 80, 93, 157
Sandys, Duncan, 40, 50
Saro-Wiwa, Ken, 131
Sauti ya Umma, 44
self-reliance, 73–74
sexual violence, 56, 77, 84, 88, 105
 against Arab, Shirazi and Asian women, 55
Shafi, Ahmada, 36, 151, 154
Shamte, Mohamed, 18, 29, 30, 31, 36, 37, 39
Shariff, Ali, 18, 30
Shariff, Othman, 30, 31, 39, 49, 54, 80

INDEX

Shein, Ali Mohamed, 101, 113, 132
Sheriff, Abdul, 11
Shirazis, 13, 14, 17, 18, 19, 27, 31, 55, 56
Shivji, Issa, 46, 47, 57, 65
Somalia, 7, 11, 109, 116, 117, 122, 133, 158, 159
Soviet Union, 17, 38, 55, 78, 117
Special Economic Zones (SEZs), 105
SWAPO, 95

T
Tanganyika African National Union (TANU), 18, 25, 27, 30, 32, 33, 63, 75, 90, 100
Tanzania People's Defense Force (TPDF), 6, 118, 121,
Tanzania Petroleum Development Corporation (TPDC), 109
Tanzanian Investment Act, 105
Toure, Sekou, 28
tourism 1, 59, 66, 102, 131, 134, 136
Twala, Abdulaziz, 44, 49, 80

U
Umma Party, 2, 3, 24, 33, 34, 42, 43, 44, 46, 53, 54, 56, 57, 58, 78, 79, 80, 81, 82, 83, 84, 85, 86, 88, 90, 92, 94, 96, 97, 134, 139–48
  dissolution of, 57–8
  launch of, 41–3
  role in Zanzibar revolution of, 47, 48, 49
United Nations, 26, 112, 157
United Nations Conference on Trade and Development (UNCTAD), 53, 54
United Nations Development Programme (UNDP), 101, 102, 127
US military, 1, 6
  and Civil Military Operations (CMOs), 6, 118, 119
  and Combined Joint Task Force–Horn of Africa (CJTF–HOA), 121
  and 'dwindling natural resources', 119
  and East African Community, 120–1
  and Joint Chiefs of Staff, 6, 47, 118
  and Joint Special Command, 122
  and Naval Forces Africa (NAVAF), 121
  role in Tanzania, 117–19

V
Venezuela, 135

W
Wakil, Idrisa Abdul, 49, 66
welfare services, 73, 103
wholesale trade, 75, 76
working class, 22, 23, 33, 41, 42

Y
Yemen, 114, 115, 116, 122, 158
Youths Own Union (YOU), 22, 23, 24

Z
Za News, 44
Zanzibar Action Plan, 2, 52
Zanzibar and Pemba Federation of Labour (ZPFL), 43
Zanzibar and Pemba People's Party (ZPPP), 31, 32, 33, 34
Zanzibar Nationalist Party (ZNP), 17, 18, 21, 22, 24, 25, 26, 27, 28, 29, 30, 31, 32, 33, 34, 35, 36, 37, 38, 39, 40, 41, 42, 43, 47, 48, 90, 133
Zanzibar Nationalist Party–Zanzibar and Pemba People's Party (ZNP–ZPPP), 35, 36, 39, 40, 42, 43, 44, 100
Zhou Enlai, 68, 71

www.ingramcontent.com/pod-product-compliance
Lightning Source LLC
Chambersburg PA
CBHW032038290426
44110CB00012B/854